THE FAITH-SHAPED LIFE

THE
FAITH-SHAPED LIFE

Ian Hamilton

THE BANNER OF TRUTH TRUST

THE BANNER OF TRUTH TRUST

3 Murrayfield Road, Edinburgh EH12 6EL, UK
P.O. Box 621, Carlisle, PA 17013, USA

*

© Ian Hamilton 2013

*

ISBN
Print: 978 1 84871 249 2
EPUB: 978 1 84871 250 8
Kindle: 978 1 84871 251 5

*

Typeset in 10/14 pt Sabon Oldstyle Figures at
the Banner of Truth Trust, Edinburgh

Printed in the USA by
Versa Press, Inc.,
East Peoria, IL

*

To my dear friends in
Loudoun Church of Scotland, Newmilns,
who supported and encouraged me
for twenty years, 1979-1999:
with my deepest gratitude.

Contents

1. Getting Started

The Christian life is a faith-shaped life. Not only is faith the instrument that unites us to Christ, it is the reality that shapes how we live in union with Christ. Writing to the Galatians, Paul declared, 'And the life I now live in the flesh I live by faith in the Son of God, who loved me and gave himself for me' (*Gal.* 2:20). Similarly in 2 Corinthians 5:7 he wrote, 'we walk (live) by faith, not by sight'. Faith, self-abandoning reliance on and trust in Jesus Christ, is the dominant motif in the Christian believer's life. This is the recurring note in Hebrews 11. It was 'by faith' that God's people 'conquered kingdoms, enforced justice, obtained promises, stopped the mouths of lions, quenched the power of fire, escaped the edge of the sword, were made strong out of weakness, became mighty in war, put foreign armies to flight' (*Heb.* 11:33, 34).

The Christian life from beginning to end is a life of faith. This does not mean that the Lord will not give his believing children tangible, even visible, tokens and expressions of his love (and anger!). It does mean, however, that the fundamental principle at the heart of the Christian life is that, like Moses, we persevere because we see him who is invisible (*Heb.* 11:27). Such sight, of course, is the sight of believing eyes, eyes opened by the Holy Spirit to see the truth and grace and glory of our Lord Jesus as he is revealed in the Holy Scriptures. 'For we live', says Paul, 'by faith, not by sight' (2 *Cor.* 5:7).

Nothing could be more basic to the Christian life than this truth. But, as Samuel Rutherford reminded us, 'It is hard to keep sight of God in a storm.' When all is well with us and ours, when God's work is going on sweetly and unhindered, when we sense the Lord's presence with us and among us, faith is drawn out easily and gladly from our hearts. But when the heavens are as brass, when God's work is assailed from without and within, when unexpected, sore, and devastating providences overtake us, faith can so easily be weakened, and at times all but eclipsed. It is deeply sobering and richly encouraging, therefore, to read the searing honesty of the Psalmist as he poured out his heart's complaints to the Lord: 'O God, why do you cast us off forever? Why does your anger smoke against the sheep of your pasture?' (*Psa.* 74:1). Even the choicest of God's servants experience spiritual desolations and trials.

There are times, as the Psalmists knew only too well, when it seems the Lord is far off, when our circumstances would suggest, and more than suggest, that God has forgotten us, or even abandoned us. We stop living by faith and start living by sight. We prefer to trust the evidence of our sinfully fallen minds and eyes rather than the promises and purposes of him who cannot lie.

Christians should never forget that it is the constant aim of Satan to persuade us to live by sight (and for that matter by feelings), rather than in glad submission to the word of God. This was Satan's tactic in the garden. Eve 'saw that the tree was good for food, and that it was a delight to the eyes . . .' (*Gen.* 3:6), and the rest is history! She preferred to live by sight and not by faith. If our first parents, sinless as they were, could be so deceived, do not think for one moment that you would never fall and do such a thing.

Another of God's choice servants, Abraham, also succumbed to living by sight and not by faith when he was persuaded to build a family through Hagar, the Egyptian maidservant, rather than wait trustingly upon God to fulfil his promise to give him a son and heir (read *Gen.* 16). And yet it is Abraham whom Paul highlights as a glorious example of a believer who lived by faith, even when all his circumstances were against him. Abraham had learned well from his failure with Hagar, and had come to live by faith and not by sight: 'No distrust made him waver concerning the promise of God, but he grew strong in his faith as he gave glory to God, fully convinced that God was able to do what he had promised' (*Rom.* 4:20, 21).

John Calvin expressed a wonderful comment on Abraham's faith at this juncture:

> Let us remember that we are all in the same condition as Abraham. Our circumstances are all in opposition to the promises of God. He promises us immortality: yet we are surrounded by mortality and corruption. He declares that He accounts us just: yet we are covered with sins. He testifies that He is propitious and benevolent towards us: yet outward signs threaten His wrath. What then are we to do? We must close our eyes, disregard ourselves and all things connected with us, so that nothing may hinder or prevent us from believing that God is true.[1]

This is what it means to live by faith and not by sight. It means to trust, no matter what, the word and promises of God, and to *act* accordingly. God is faithful. He is altogether trustworthy. That is the message of the cross. He has given us his best and highest in the Lord Jesus Christ and he will withhold no lesser blessing (*Rom.* 8:32). Believe it. Be sure of it. The cross is the guarantee of it.

The aim of this book, therefore, is to flesh out what it means to 'live by faith'. The Christian life is not an easy life. Our Saviour warned us that in this world we

[1] *Calvin's Commentaries: The Epistles of Paul The Apostle to the Romans and to the Thessalonians*, eds. David W Torrance and T. F. Torrance (Edinburgh, 1961), p. 99.

would experience tribulations (*John* 16:33). He told us that just as the world had hated him, so also it would hate those who belonged to him (*John* 15:18ff.). The Christian finds himself or herself in unrelenting warfare with the world, the flesh and the devil. Every step forward in Christ-likeness will be contested. The one thing that will keep us on track and pressing on is moment by moment trust in God, in his word, in the goodness and perfection of his purposes, and in his 'exceedingly great and precious' promises, which 'find their Yes in him [Christ]' (2 *Cor.* 1:20). Indeed, 'this is the victory that has overcome the world—our faith' (*1 John* 5:4).

The following chapters are intentionally brief. However, my hope is that they will provide enough biblical teaching to encourage and challenge both younger and older Christians; and above all to point us relentlessly to Jesus Christ 'the founder and perfecter of our faith' (*Heb.* 12:2). For this reason, our onward progress in the life of faith depends on us grasping the truth that the strength and glory of faith lies not in anything in us, but wholly in our Lord Jesus Christ. Biblical faith fundamentally looks out and up, not in and around. Grasping this will do more than anything to liberate us from the tyranny of self, even a redeemed self, and help us to see that Christ is all.

2. Faith: An Overused and Much Misunderstood Word

'Faith' is perhaps the most used word in the evangelical vocabulary. Without faith it is impossible to please God (*Heb.* 11:6). The righteousness of God comes through faith in Jesus Christ for all who believe (*Rom.* 3:22). It is by faith that we stand firm. We are to resist the devil firm in our faith (*1 Pet.* 5:9). We are to take up the shield of faith so that we might extinguish all the flaming darts of the evil one (*Eph.* 6:16). It is our faith that overcomes the world (*1 John* 5:4). Indeed, we walk by faith, not by sight (*2 Cor.* 5:7). Faith is basic and absolutely essential to authentic Christianity. The Bible could not be any clearer or more emphatic in its teaching on faith.

There is, however, a problem that needs to be addressed. When many Christians think about 'faith', their tendency is to think first about the *quality* of their faith and not about the *object* of their faith. This leads to a skewing of the Christian life and a lack of personal assurance. I do not mean that we should never reflect on the quality of our faith. Our Saviour rebuked his disciples for their 'little faith'. My concern rather is to make the point that faith, to quote Prof. John Murray, is 'essentially extraspective'.[1] Murray's telling phrase

[1] John Murray, *The Epistle to the Romans* (London, 1960), p. 123.

highlights the primary movement of true faith. It does not look into self, it is not principially 'introspective'; it looks out and away to the Lord Jesus Christ. He is the focus of faith. Who he is and what he has done is the place where faith casts its anchor for the soul.

To grasp this basic, indeed very basic, fact, will transform our lives. It is undoubtedly one of the devil's stratagems to turn the Christian in upon himself (*incurvatus in se*, to use Luther's words). Once he gets us preoccupied with looking in, the clouds of our many sins and failures hide the precious and perfect justifying righteousness of the Lord Jesus from our view. We fret over the inconstancy of our faith. We become distressed by the shallowness of our faith. We are humbled by the coldness of our faith. You may now already be asking: 'But is it not right and good that we do this?' Yes . . . and no! Yes, if we do it 'looking to Jesus, the founder and perfecter of our faith' (*Heb.* 12:2). But if we do it with both eyes on ourselves, the devil will cast us into the deepest of pits. The words of John Rogers, the early English Puritan, are always timely:

> Weak faith is true faith—as precious, though not as great as strong faith: the same Holy Ghost the author, the same Gospel the instrument . . . For it is not the strength of our faith that saves, but the truth of our faith—not the weakness of our faith that condemns, but the want [lack]—of faith.

Faith is 'essentially extraspective'. Faith's first glance

is to Christ. But no less is faith's continuing glances focused on Christ too. Faith is nourished, not by looking in to find crumbs of spiritual comfort, but by looking out and feeding on the 'Bread of Life'. He is our great encouragement. His love to me, not my love to him, supports my soul. His faithfulness to me, not my faithfulness to him, will bring me safely home.

In no sense am I seeking to diminish the importance of spiritual responsibility. We are called to 'add to our faith' and to 'grow in faith'. But first, we are called to fix our eyes on 'Jesus, the founder and perfecter of our faith' (*Heb.* 12:2).

Where are you looking as you read this? Where am I looking? May the Lord give us all the grace, and the wisdom to look out and up (I am speaking theologically, not spatially!), fixing our eyes on Jesus, who is the 'Alpha and the Omega', the beginning and the end (*Rev.* 1:8).

3. The Holy Trinity: Faith's Constant Delight

What would you say is the fundamental doctrine of the Christian Faith? For many of us the instinctive answer would be, 'justification by faith alone, in Christ alone'. There is no doubt, or should be no doubt, that this is a biblical and evangelical fundamental. Martin Luther described justification by faith alone, in Christ alone, as 'The article of a standing or falling church', and rightly so. John Calvin called it 'the hinge on which true religion turns'. We surely understand what Luther and Calvin were saying: could anything be more important than knowing how God brings judgment-deserving sinners into a right and reconciled relationship with himself? This is why we cannot in any way endorse any collaboration of evangelicals with Roman Catholics in this vital area of biblical truth. The theological 'fudge' that such collaboration in recent years has resulted in is worthy of Trent (the sixteenth-century Roman Catholic Church Council that anathematised the Protestant doctrine of justification through faith alone, in Christ alone). Justification by faith alone, in Christ alone, is too precious to compromise in the interests of a false ecumenism. True church unity is never served by fudging God's truth in the interests of ecclesiastical peace!

Equally surely, however, we cannot say that justification by faith alone is *the* fundamental doctrine of the Christian Faith. That honour rightly and surely belongs to the doctrine of the Trinity. God himself is the fundamental truth of the Christian Faith. He is Truth itself. He is the Creator, Sustainer, Initiator, and Sovereign Lord of all that is. God does not exist for us, we exist for him. Paul's declaration in Romans 11:36 wonderfully makes the point: 'For from him and through him and to him are all things. To him be glory for ever. Amen.'

Think for a moment about the glorious doctrine of justification by grace alone, through faith alone, in Christ alone. The Christ, by whose blood we have been justified (*Rom.* 5:10), accomplished his saving work from womb to tomb as the Father's Servant, upheld by the Holy Spirit (*Isa.* 42:1ff; *Heb.* 9:14). Not for one moment did he act independently. In all he did, the Father and the Spirit were actively present. Certainly it was not the Father or the Spirit who became incarnate and suffered on Calvary's cross. But it was the Spirit who upheld the Saviour in his mediatorial work, and it was 'through the eternal Spirit that [he] offered himself without blemish to God' (*Heb.* 9:14). Our salvation was accomplished in perfect harmony by the holy Trinity, acting in concert. Undergirding the whole fabric of creation in general and the work of salvation in particular are the three persons of the Godhead. God the Trinity is first and last.

The pre-eminence of God's triune being is heralded in a number of ways in the Scriptures. In Genesis 1, we see the Triune God in creation: God, his Word, and his Spirit, together bringing into being worlds and star systems out of nothing, and creating man and woman in their own image. Who we are is a personal, visual, and constant reminder to us of our existence, and of the priority of the Triune God.

It is surely not without significance that God should

disclose the Tri-unity of his being to us in the Bible's opening chapter. All that is has its being from, and is a reflection of, the Triune God. In the New Testament, we see the Triune God working in harmony to accomplish the salvation of sinners: the Father purposing, the Son saving, and the Spirit applying (though all three actively work at every moment and at every phase of redemption—*opera ad extra trinitatis indivisa sunt*—the works of the Trinity outside itself are indivisible). Our salvation flows from and owes everything to the eternal fellowship of Father, Son and Holy Spirit.

The writer to the Hebrews wonderfully highlights the Trinitarian quality and character of Christian salvation when he speaks of Christ offering himself through the eternal Spirit to God (*Heb.* 9:14). Further, we see our Lord Jesus in John 17:21, praying that his church will be patterned after the harmony and inter-dependent unity of the Trinity. God's Tri-unity, his essential harmony and mutual indwelling, is what the church is to be modelled on. If nothing else, living more in conscious awareness of God's essential disclosure as triune, will in some measure (surely), compel us to be 'eager to maintain the unity of the Spirit in the bond of peace' (*Eph.* 4:3).

We could go on at length, showing how the truth of the Trinity is woven into the very fabric of biblical revelation, of Christian salvation, of the church's life, and of the individual believer's growth in grace.

And yet, is it not true that Bible-believing Christians, in general, think so little about the Trinity? Is it not a fact, deeply to be lamented, that our lives are so little framed by this most fundamental of all biblical truths? The opening verses of John's Gospel introduce to us the unspeakably glorious reality of God's triune being, and to its unfathomableness. Before all worlds existed, before anything was, God was! And, staggeringly, he was a community, a fellowship; 'and the Word was with [face to face with] God'! The Father was with the Son, and the Son was with the Father. And together they were with the Holy Spirit. 'In the beginning', an eternal fellowship of holy love and loving holiness 'was'. We 'become', the Trinity 'was'. Here, if anywhere, we are on holy ground. We speak, only so that we may not be silent (to quote Augustine). Here we are quite out of our depth. But yet it is precisely here, that we cultivate that humility of mind that keeps us from becoming insufferably proud in our knowledge of God. Here, if anywhere, we are cut down to size.

John Calvin tells us (*Institutes* 1.13.17) of a passage in the writings of Gregory Nazianzen that, he said, 'vastly delights me':

> No sooner do I conceive of the One than I am illumined by the splendour of the Three; no sooner do I distinguish them than I am carried back to the One. When I think of any one of the Three I think of him as the whole, and my eyes are filled, and the greater part of what I am thinking escapes me.

Can you relate in any way to Gregory or Calvin? Does

the truth of the Holy Trinity 'vastly delight' you?

What time do you give to pondering the revealed glory of our Triune, Saviour God? What honour do we ascribe, in our personal and corporate worship as the church, to the Persons, being and actings of our Triune God? The Christian faith rests upon and centres in the Triune God: 'For from him and through him and to him are all things. To him be the glory for ever! Amen'.

4. *The Catholicity of Faith*

Of all people, Christians, and Reformed Christians in particular, have the least to be proud about. In rebuking some Christians in Corinth for their pride, Paul exclaimed, 'What do you have that you did not receive? If then you received it, why do you boast as if you did not receive it?' (*1 Cor.* 4:7). What have we indeed to boast about? Were we not 'dead in our trespasses' when God in his grace 'made us alive together with Christ'? (*Eph.* 2:5). Were we not guilty, hell-deserving sinners, God's very enemies, when he showed his love for us and gave up the Lord Jesus Christ to die that sin-bearing, wrath-quenching death of the cross to deliver us from a ruined eternity and bring us ultimately to glory? (*Rom.* 5:8). Total depravity and unconditional election are not merely doctrines to confess, they are truths to humble us to the dust. And yet, how easily, only too easily, can we allow our vast gospel privileges and blessings to turn us into self-regarding, narrow-hearted men and women.

One incident in the Gospels illustrates the point. John the disciple saw a man driving out 'demons in your [Jesus'] name and we told him to stop, because he was not following us' (*Mark* 9:38). Not one of us! Jesus' response was swift and categorical: 'Do not stop him . . .' The disciples had become narrow-hearted and exclusive. After all, they were *Christ's* disciples, *his* hand-picked apostles. They were *the men*. And anyway, who was this stranger who was casting out demons in Jesus' name? 'He was not one of us', of that much John and the others were sure. An exclusive spirit had overtaken the disciples; this man did not belong to their privileged group and so they told him to stop what he was doing. The man, however, was clearly doing a good work; he was fighting on the same side as John and the others. He was not in their little group, but he belonged to Jesus!

What are we to make of this incident? J. C. Ryle had this to say:

Here is a golden rule indeed, and one that human nature sorely needs, and has too often forgotten. Men of all branches of Christ's Church are apt to think that no good can be done in the world, unless it is done by their own party and denomination. They are so narrow-minded, that they cannot conceive the possibility of working on any other pattern but that which they follow. They make an idol of their own peculiar ecclesiastical machinery, and can see no merit in any other.[1]

Ryle is not saying, and I am not saying, that Christians should turn a blind eye to sin and evil in other Christians (though we have a marked propensity to see clearly in others what we are blind to in ourselves read *Matt.* 7:1ff.). But we must diligently guard our churches from becoming infected with a self-preening, self-regarding spirit, that imagines we are the people and wisdom will die with us (*Job* 12:1)! We must see beyond ourselves to all who are fighting the good fight of the faith and warring against our great enemy, the devil. We must cultivate a brotherly spirit towards all who love the Lord Jesus Christ in sincerity and truth.

Of course there will be tensions and difficulties! We all have cherished and prized distinctives. And I have no doubt that it is ten thousand times easier to commend and preach this than to practise it, but practise this we must. What else is the Holy Spirit teaching us from this Gospel incident? The fundamental issue is not, Is he one of *us*?, but, Is he one of *Christ's*? If nothing else, such large-heartedness will help save us from self-righteous

[1] J. C. Ryle, *Expository Thoughts on the Gospels: Mark* (Edinburgh: Banner of Truth, 2012), p. 150.

censoriousness towards fellow blood-bought brothers and sisters. Our differences will no doubt remain, but the spirit in which we engage in our differences will honour our Saviour.

The faith that honours Christ is a 'wide-angled' faith, a faith that sees beyond itself and embraces all whom Christ in his grace has embraced. Such faith refuses to make denominational allegiance its theological default for cultivating fellowship. It instinctively seeks out everyone whom the Saviour himself has sought out.

Do you recognise yourself? More can and must be said; less would make us holier than God. May God give us the grace to see other Christians with the eyes and heart of Christ.

5. Specks and Logs: Faith and Judging Others

Our Lord Jesus' teaching is always deeply searching, sometimes almost unbearably so. Few statements of our Lord are more calculated to search out our hearts than what he says about 'specks' and 'logs' (*Matt.* 7:1-5). The picture conveyed by our Lord is almost comical. A man with a huge log of wood sticking out of his eye says to another man who is troubled by a speck of wood in his eye, 'Let me take the speck out of your eye.' There is no doubt the man with the speck in his eye needs help. The speck needs to be removed, before it causes him greater problems. It is a little problem, but it is a real problem, and needs removing. But who is to remove the speck? Certainly not the man with the log sticking out of his eye! Of all people, he is least suited and fitted to do the job. Why? Because, while he sees that the man with the speck has a problem, he is blind to the even greater problems in his own life. His 'log' has blinded him, made him insensible, to his own great need. In trying to take the speck out of the other man's eye (if his log would even allow him to know what and where the speck was!), the man with the log would do great damage.

Jesus is not saying that 'specks' don't matter. Everything in our lives matters to God. If there are things wrong in our lives they need to be dealt with and removed. When Jesus says in Matthew 7:1, 'Judge not, that you be not judged', his words have often been misunderstood. Our Lord is not saying absolutely that we are not to judge. Indeed, in verse 6 Jesus encourages us to make judgments: 'Do not give dogs what is holy and do not throw your pearls to pigs'! What, then, does Jesus mean? His illustration is surely obvious: the man with the log sticking out of his eye is the man who sees only too clearly sins in others, but is acutely blind to recognising, far less acknowledging, the sin in his own life. Indeed, he is blind to the fact that the sin in his life is greater than anything he sees in the lives of others. He is a 'censorious man'. This was one of the besetting sins of the Pharisees. They were past masters at seeing sin in others while being utterly oblivious to their own sin: no wonder Jesus called them 'blind guides' (*Matt.* 23:16).

This spirit of censoriousness is only too common among professing Christians. We can all, only too easily, slip into this self-exalting sin. What is often missed, however, is the fact that the censor usually has a point. There are specks, lots of them, and they need pointing out and removing—but not by those who are 'holier than thou'. In pastoral ministry, and all Christians are pastors to one another, the application of truth is not the only objective. We are told of our Lord Jesus, 'A bruised reed he will not break, and a faintly burning wick he will not quench' (*Isa.* 42:3). 'He knows our frame; he remembers we are dust'! (*Psa.* 103:14). The spirit in which we comfort, counsel, and rebuke one another is of paramount importance.

Paul urges Timothy to correct his opponents with 'gentleness' (2 *Tim.* 2:25). He reminds the censorious Corinthians, 'Love is patient and kind; love does not envy or boast; it is not arrogant or rude. It does not insist on its own way; it is not irritable or resentful; it does not rejoice at wrongdoing, but rejoices with the truth' (*1 Cor.* 13:4-6).

In pointing out the sins of others, boldness is usually needed, and many of us shrink from that. But no less is tenderness needed; the tenderness of the One who was so extraordinarily patient and forbearing with his errant and slow to learn disciples.

It's not hard to see 'specks'—they are everywhere. It's also not hard to see 'logs', except when it's your own log. May the Lord preserve us all from 'holier than God' spirituality. Such 'spirituality' has at least one distinguishing feature—it prizes the 'head' more than the 'heart'. Of course, they belong together, the former nourishing the latter. But only too easily, as we see in Scripture and in the history of the church, they can be separated—and when they are, spirituality becomes metallic and clinical.

The most effective antidote to such censoriousness is conformity to our Lord Jesus. None were holier than he, none were gentler than he. So Paul could write, 'Be kind to one another, tenderhearted, forgiving one another, as God in Christ forgave you. Therefore be imitators of God, as beloved children . . .' (*Eph.* 4:32-5:1)

6. Faith and Christian Unity

The church of Jesus Christ is an international, multi-cultural fellowship of believers. In the Book of Revelation, John is given a vision of the church's ultimate glory in God's nearer presence. What he saw was 'a great multitude that no one could number, from every nation, from all tribes and peoples and languages, standing before the throne and before the Lamb' (*Rev.* 7:9). It is a picture of multi-coloured, variegated harmony; a picture of the worshipping oneness that marks the life of God's redeemed people. This is what the church one day will be. This is the ordained omega point for the church. What we so often forget, however, is that the church's oneness is not only its future destiny, it is its present reality—really!

In a Christian world marked and marred by a multitude of denominations, and splits from denominations, and splits from splits, we have all but lost sight of the great biblical truth that believers 'are all one in Christ Jesus' (*Gal.* 3:28). Paul is not writing here of some future hope; he says we 'are, now, presently, all one in Christ Jesus'. He is not engaging in some flight of theological fancy, he has not taken leave of his senses; he is speaking the sober truth. We 'are all one in Christ Jesus'.

You don't need to have an acute theological mind to realise how breathtaking Paul's statement is. Look around you. Look at your own church, and the other evangelical churches in your area. Look beyond your own limited horizon to the evangelical churches throughout your land—'all one in Christ Jesus'? Doesn't Paul's declaration smack of empty sloganeering? The fragmented nature of the evangelical witness and our divisions and sub-divisions, appear to mock the apostle's inspired words. But this is Holy Scripture; 'you are all one in Christ Jesus'.

What does Paul mean? Simply this: God has but one church, the body and bride of his Son. Our Lord Jesus has only one body and one bride. There is only 'one Lord, one faith, one baptism; one God and Father of all, who is over all and through all and in all' (*Eph.* 4:5, 6). There is only one salvation which is by grace alone, though faith alone, in Jesus Christ alone. There is only one Holy Spirit who indwells, equally, every true believer in Christ, however wrong-headed some of their thinking is. There is only one Bible, which every true believer believes and loves and obeys. Christian unity is not an illusion, it is a fact.

Remember, however, we are talking about *Christian* unity; we are all one 'in Christ Jesus'. Our Lord Jesus is the basis and boundary of truly Christian unity. Beyond faith in him as the 'only Mediator between man and God', there is no unity.

Our Lord Jesus prayed, 'that they [his church] may be one even as we are one, I in them and you in me, that they may become perfectly one, so that the world may know that you sent me and loved them even as you loved me' (*John* 17:22, 23). Our Saviour prayed this. What are you, what am I, doing by his grace to realise this? I have no easy answers. But I am persuaded that until we acknowledge our lamentable failures to practise the unity that is ours in Christ, we continue to sin grievously against our God. Take these words of John Owen to heart:

I confess I would rather, much rather, spend all my time and days in making up and healing the breaches and schisms that are amongst Christians than one hour in justifying our divisions, even therein wherein, on the one side, they are capable of a fair defence . . . When men have laboured as much in the principle of forbearance as they have done to subdue other men to their opinions, religion will have another appearance in the world.[1]

Listen to John Murray,

. . . the lack of unity among the churches of Christ which profess the faith in its purity is a patent violation of the unity of the body of Christ . . . We cannot escape the implications for us by resorting to the notion of the invisible church. The body of Christ is not an invisible entity, and the prayer of Jesus was directed to the end that the world might believe . . . The implications for visible confession and witness are unavoidable.[2]

I cannot but think that if we saw other believers for what they truly were, the Father's blood-bought children, people indwelt by Christ himself, loved, redeemed, elected sinners, we would treat one another

[1] John Owen, *Works of John Owen* (Edinburgh: Banner of Truth, 1965-8), 13:95.
[2] John Murray, *Collected Writings* (Edinburgh: Banner of Truth, 1977), 2:335

quite differently. If God has made them 'clean', we dare not call them 'common' (nor treat them as common).

Too often we make ourselves the measure of all things and exclude all who do not dot all our 'i's and cross all our 't's. Our Father is more generous and merciful. This is not a plea for Christians to close their eyes and shut their ears to error that needs reproving. It is rather a plea for all of us to remember that 'love covers a multitude of sins'—for which all of us, I trust, are and will be eternally thankful.

7. *Faith and Disappointment*

One of the first things a young believer discovers is that the life of faith is not immune from the disappointments and heartaches of what Paul calls 'the sufferings of this present time' (*Rom.* 8:18). God does not exempt his children from unexpected, sorely wounding providences. In 2 Corinthians 1:8, Paul tells us that the hardships and pressures he and his friends were experiencing were so severe, that 'we despaired of life itself'!

Even in *the* model life of faith, we find our Lord Jesus Christ experiencing disappointment, opposition, hardships, and bereavement. Nowhere does God imply that his believing children will be cocooned from the struggles, disappointments, and perplexities of living in a fallen world. On the contrary, the Lord tells us that 'all who desire to live a godly life in Christ Jesus will be persecuted' (2 *Tim.* 3:12). Without this spiritual realism, our lives will become the prisoners of circumstance, rising and falling depending on the kind of circumstances that touch us.

But the Lord has given us infinitely more than the grace of spiritual realism in order that we might cope with the heartaches, disappointments, and mysteries that inevitably cross our path.

First of all, he promises us his unfailing presence in all our times of need: 'I will never leave you nor forsake you' (*Heb.* 13:5). More than that, he promises to be the indwelling helper of his children. In the upper room, as he faced the cross, the Lord Jesus assured his disciples, 'I will not leave you as orphans; I will come to you' (*John* 14:18). He was speaking of his coming in his Spirit to be their abiding indwelling Sanctifier and Friend. Whatever difficulties and disappointments you face, however sore God's unexpected providences, of this you can be sure, you are *never alone!* All the resources of the Godhead are for you and in you. Believe this.

More than this, God assures us that not one unexpected providence that touches his children's lives is fortuitous. Our God is the One 'who works all things according to the counsel of his will' (*Eph.* 1:11). Here we come face to face with God's unconditional sovereignty. But this truth is revealed in Scripture not as a puzzle to unravel, but as a comfort to embrace. Who is this God who is unconditionally sovereign over all things? He is the God who 'did not spare his own Son but gave him up for us all' (*Rom.* 8:32). He is 'the Father of mercies and God of all comfort' (2 *Cor.* 1:3). It is our loving heavenly Father who does whatsoever he pleases. Who God is to us in Christ is our assurance that

> My Father's hand will never cause
> His child a needless tear.[1]

Believe this. By faith, draw out the comfort of being a dearly loved and precious child of a sovereign and loving Father.

There is yet another strand of encouragement that God gives to us in his word. In 2 Corinthians 1, where Paul recounts the great pressures that were causing him to despair even of life, he tells us, 'this was to make us rely not on ourselves but on God who raises the dead' (2 *Cor.* 1:9). God was pleased to bring his servant into such straitened circumstances in order to strengthen his trust and confirm his obedience.

Samuel Rutherford made the same point: 'Faith is the better for the free air and the sharp winter storm in its face. Grace withereth without adversity.'[2] God always has our eternal as well as our present good in mind in his relations with us.

---

[1] From William F. Lloyd's hymn, 'My times are in Thy hand.'
[2] Samuel Rutherford, *Letters of Samuel Rutherford* (Edinburgh: Banner of Truth, 1984), p. 290.

John Newton's celebrated hymn, 'These Inward Trials', captures the grace of God's dealings with his hard-pressed children. Having asked the Lord for growth in 'faith and love and every grace', the child of God finds his life assaulted on all sides by unexpected and sore providences. In response to the Christian's perplexity at what has happened, the Lord replies:

> These inward trials I employ,
>   From self and pride to set thee free,
> And break thy schemes of earthly joy,
>   That thou mayest seek thy all in Me.[1]

The Lord always and ever has our best before him. He is 'the gardener' who lovingly prunes the branches united to the true vine so that they will 'bear more fruit' (see *John* 15:1, 2).

Until we go to be with the Lord, we will find unexpected and sore providences touching our lives. It cannot be otherwise, for the servant is not greater than his master. But, though we might well be hard pressed on every side, we are never crushed. Though we might well be perplexed, we are never in despair. Even if we are persecuted, we are never abandoned (see 2 *Cor.* 4:8, 9). God will not exempt you, his beloved child, from tears or pains; but he will be with you, and in you, every step of the way, bringing the infinite resources of the Godhead graciously to sustain you and make you

[1] The first line of this hymn by Newton is, 'I asked the Lord that I might grow'.

more than conqueror (*Rom.* 8:39). He who promised is faithful. Here is where faith casts it anchor, in the undeniable faithfulness of God in Christ. So, even though our faith is weak and at times tottering, it is securely fixed in God, the One who cannot be shaken.

8. *The Anchor that Keeps Faith Steadfast*

One of the most significant growth points in the believer's life is the dawning realisation that Christian doctrine matters for Christian living. How we live as God's children will be shaped by the impact of God's truth upon our minds and hearts. This is so basic; and yet it can hardly be denied that many Christians languish in the shadows of God's love when they should be basking in the noon-day sunshine of his love, and all because they fail to make the connection between believing the truth and enjoying the truth.

This is perhaps nowhere more evident than in the lack of assurance that blights the lives of many Christians. Lack of assurance is due to many reasons. But is it not true, that for many, if not all, lack of assurance that we are truly Christ's is due to a failure to think through the implications of one of the gospel's foundational doctrines, justification by faith alone in Christ alone?

Consider Paul's glorious conclusion to his exposition of God's justifying righteousness in Romans 5:1; 'Therefore, since we have been justified by faith, we have peace with God through our Lord Jesus Christ.' Having put our trust alone in Jesus Christ, 'the Lord our righteousness', 'we have peace with God'. It is a once for all, eternally settled fact. God is at peace with us and we are at peace with him. No longer does he count our sins against us—he has counted them all against Christ. No longer are we under God's wrath—Christ exhausted his wrath against us by his sin-bearing death on the cross. No longer do we face the nightmare prospect of being forever banished from God's presence in hell—Christ took our banishment upon himself and went into 'the far country', that we might never be separated from God. This is what it means to be 'justified': to be, by faith alone, in the saving work of Christ alone, eternally and irreversibly right with God. This means that the weakest, most stumbling believer is no less justified than the Apostle Paul or John Calvin or Jonathan Edwards or William Carey! Is this not the sweetest and most reassuring of truths? Of course, it can be abused. But the abuse of it does not detract from the truth and glory of it.

Now, do you see the connection between Christian doctrine and Christian living? Every believer is at 'peace with God'. Augustus Toplady put the issue memorably in his glorious hymn 'A Debtor to Mercy Alone':

> More happy, but not more secure,
>   the glorified spirits in heaven.

This is a truth every Christian needs to ponder and out of which to suck the strongest encouragement. It is little wonder that Martin Luther called justification by faith 'The article of a standing or falling church.' He could equally have said that it is the 'Article of a standing or falling Christian.'

This is why we should be deeply concerned about the near eclipse of doctrine in modern day evangelicalism. The spiritual fallout from doctrine less Christianity (if such a thing exists at all!) is, and cannot but be, immense. When our Christian life is not securely anchored to the mighty, unrepeatable, saving acts of God, we become a prey, not only to 'every wind of doctrine', but to the deceits of the devil and the fluctuating moods of our temperaments. We begin to look for signs of assurance in our experiences, in our feelings, in happy providences. Our spiritual gaze becomes narcissistic: what I am, not what God has done in Christ, becomes the controlling focus of my life. Assurance becomes almost a quest for self-validation, not a rejoicing in the finished work of Christ and the grace of justifying righteousness.

It is a constant ploy of the devil to absorb us with ourselves; to turn the Christian faith into an exercise in the acquiring of self-esteem. Our great weapon against his insidious self-promoting, Christ-dishonouring tactics, is to live out the connection between God's justification of the ungodly through faith alone in Jesus Christ, and the relationship every believer now enjoys with God on account of that: 'Therefore, since we have been justified by faith, we have peace with God through our Lord Jesus Christ.'

Christian doctrine matters for Christian living. That was once an evangelical commonplace. Is it a truth that shapes and styles how you live? Are you learning to suck the sweet marrow of blessedness from gospel doctrines? The proof that you are will not be a swollen head, but an enlarged heart.

9. *What Faith Looks Like*

One of the most deeply moving, and constantly recurring features in the Bible is God's unyielding commitment to his covenant people. It is altogether breathtaking to see God's enduring faithfulness to a people who were in turn rebellious, disobedient, forgetful, and plain ungrateful towards him. This unyielding faithfulness is graphically illustrated in the Israelites' confession of sin recorded in Nehemiah 9. As they survey their spiritually-chequered history, and especially their wilful defections from their covenant Lord, the people plead the enduring faithfulness and grace of his character: 'But you are a forgiving God, gracious and compassionate, slow to anger and abounding in love. Therefore you did not desert them, even when they cast for themselves an image of a calf and said, "This is your god, who brought you up out of Egypt", or when they committed awful blasphemies.' These are astonishing words. Of course, as Paul discovered, such unfettered grace can be used as an excuse for living lawless or antinomian lives (read *Rom.* 6:1ff.). To the child of God, however, the grace of God's character, far from being an excuse to go on sinning, is the greatest incentive to hate sin and, with the Spirit's help, to put sin to death in his life.

It is true, however, that God reveals the grace of his character not merely for our admiration, but also for our emulation. What Paul writes to Christians in Ephesus brings us face to face with the life believers are called to in our union with Jesus Christ: 'Be kind and compassionate to one another, forgiving each other, just as in Christ God forgave you. Be imitators of God, therefore, as dearly loved children . . .' (*Eph.* 4:32-5:1). We are to treat one another with the same patience, forbearance, generosity, and kindness with which the Lord has treated us. We are to mirror and reflect in our lives something of the 'family likeness'. This is daunting, to say the least. And yet, this is the life that every Christian is called to; this *is* the life of faith.

This high and holy calling to be imitators of God in the way we treat one another (face to face and when speaking with others!), is pressed upon the Ephesian

Christians by Paul (read *Eph.* 4:1, 2). What is so important for us to grasp is the reason why Paul so passionately urges Christians to 'bear with one another in love': do so, he says, to 'Maintain the unity of the Spirit in the bond of peace.' Christian unity was not a marginal doctrine for Paul. Nor was it something that was of peripheral concern to him. Christian unity for Paul was of paramount importance. It was his concern to guard Christian unity, the unity that all believers have through union with Jesus Christ, that prompted Paul to urge God's people to 'be completely humble and gentle' and 'be patient, bearing with one another in love' (*Eph.* 4:2). As he lies chained in a Roman prison, the apostle's heart pleads for God's own people to cherish their unity in Christ and to do all they can to preserve and beautify that Spirit-wrought unity.

Never has the church more needed to hear and heed these words. We live in a world obsessed with its own rights. The 'pick and mix' character of consumerism has invaded the life of the church and all but absolutised the 'rights' and desires of individual believers to pursue their own concerns with little regard for other Christians. The slogans of society's gurus are increasingly heard within professing Bible-believing churches: 'Be true to yourself'; 'Find your own space'; 'Develop a positive self-image'; 'Recover self-esteem.' If Christians are listening to society's 'self-image gurus' it is little wonder that the evangelical church is so fragmented, self-absorbed, and increasingly a stranger to the objective, abidingly true and life-enriching doctrines of Holy Scripture. Didn't our Lord Jesus Christ tell us that we would find our life only if we lost it; that only if we denied ourselves and took up our cross could we follow him? (read *Mark* 8:34, 35).

Self-absorption lies at the root of much that scars the life and witness of our Saviour's church today. Forgetting ourselves and seeking the good of others is not only healthy, it is a spiritual grace that helps to 'maintain the unity of the Spirit in the bond of peace',

Guarding the unity of the Spirit for Christ's sake is the call that comes to every Christian. So, says Paul, 'Get rid of all bitterness, rage and anger, brawling and slander' — and he is writing to Christians! — 'along with every form of malice. Be kind and compassionate to one another, forgiving each other, just as in Christ God forgave you. Be imitators of God, therefore, as dearly loved children.'

10. *The Brotherliness of Faith*

Some years ago I came across this striking comment from one of the early Church Fathers, Theophylact: 'It is a matter of shame to Christians, that while the devil can persuade wicked men to lay aside their enmities in order to do harm, Christians cannot even keep up friendship in order to do good.' Theophylact was commenting on Pilate and Herod laying aside their enmity and becoming friends (*Luke* 23:12). It could hardly be doubted by any thoughtful Christian that the ancient Father was speaking the truth. Thomas Brooks, the eminently readable Puritan, said something very similar: 'It is a natural thing for a wolf to worry a lamb; but it is a monstrous and unnatural thing for a lamb to worry another lamb.'

Why do Christians find it so hard to practise the brotherly love that our Saviour said would mark us out as being his (*John* 13:35)? No doubt the reasons are as many as there are Christians! But some reasons in particular are obvious to us all. In the first place, we are too denominationally minded. We talk too much about being Baptists, Presbyterians, Methodists, Anglicans, and the like. Don't misunderstand me: I am a convinced Presbyterian and a passionately committed paedo-baptist. I am always amazed that my fellow believers don't see the wisdom and grace of these truths! But while these are precious truths to me, the word of God reminds me that there are no Presbyterians in heaven (nor Baptists for that matter), only Christians. It is surely possible for us to hold fast to our distinctives, without un-churching those believers who do not, and to cultivate that largeness of spirit which embraces all whom God in his grace embraces—unless, of course, we are holier than God!

Before believers are anything else, they are Christians, members of the family of the living God, bound together in that divine family with a countless multitude of sinners saved by grace, blood-bought brothers and sisters.

A second reason why Christians can be less than generous-hearted to one another, is our tendency to major on doctrinal correctness. Again, don't misunderstand me. We can never be too much concerned to believe the truth, love the truth, practise the truth, and commend the truth. What, then, do I mean? Simply this: the New Testament takes heresy of the heart every bit as seriously as heresy of the head. A. A. Hodge, son of Charles Hodge, wrote,

> Zeal for doctrine has in too many instances been narrow and prejudiced, mingled with the infirmities of personal pride and party spirit, and has hence led to the unnecessary divisions and alienations of those who were in reality one in faith, and to the conditioning of communion, and even of salvation, upon unessential points.

James Alexander, another of old Princeton's theological giants, wrote, 'At the judgment I heartily believe that some heresies of heart and temper will be charged as worse than heavy doctrinal errors.' When, however, did you last hear of a Christian being disciplined for lovelessness, gossip, back-biting, or envy? It is only too possible for us to be doctrinally on the ball, to be 'reformed', and yet have cold, loveless hearts, so showing that we are not true Christians (read *1 John* 4:7-12, 20, 21). When God's truth breaks into our lives, it not only informs and reforms our minds, it also melts our hearts and transforms our lives. Take the Apostle Paul's words to heart: 'Do nothing from rivalry or conceit, but in humility count others more significant than yourselves . . . Have this mind among yourselves which is yours in Christ Jesus . . .' (*Phil.* 2:3-5). Paul proceeds to highlight the self-denying humility of the Saviour as he pursued our everlasting good.

Is it nothing short of scandalous the way some Christians speak and write about their fellow believers? It would do us well daily to breathe the air of Galatians 5:22, 23: 'The fruit of the Spirit is love, joy, peace, patience, kindness, goodness, faithfulness, gentleness, self-control.' If these Christ-like graces are not in some measure marking our lives and our relationships, our heads may well be filled with truth, but our hearts will be as yet unregenerate.

A third reason why Christians are not the friends they could and should be, is fear. 'The fear of man brings a snare', says Solomon. Too often Christians are influenced by what 'others will think'. Again, don't misunderstand me. It is right that we consider the impact our words and actions will have on other Christians. But there is a tyranny that some Christians never escape from, the tyranny of fearing the displeasure of 'important' believers (*Gal.* 2:11-14). And so, we narrow our circle of friends and curtail our range of spiritual engagements, in order not to offend those of a less catholic spirit. Again let me say, is it not possible for us to hold passionately to our biblical and theological distinctives, and at the same time practise that largeness of heart and spirit that marks the character of the God of grace? Too often some Christians are more concerned not to get things wrong, than to get things right. Those two attitudes produce two very different Christian lifestyles: one is cramped and defensive, while the other is generous and catholic-spirited.

A recent book on the church, has the striking title, *You in Your Small Corner*.[1] One of the author's concerns is to put a biblical sword into the pettiness and narrowness that so often tragically marks the life and attitudes of Christians. The church, God's saved people, is his family. We are not to live in isolated small corners, but in inter-acting, loving fellowship. This is easier said than done. It will take effort, generosity, frankness, courage, and above all humility. We will never all agree about everything: we don't need to! But we do need to learn to disagree in ways that 'maintain the unity of the Spirit in the bonds of peace'. We do need to speak to one another, and about one another, in ways that honour the Christ we serve and the people he loves. We need to look fellow Christians in the face and see Christ. In other words, let's be friends!

[1] Mark Johnston, *You In Your Small Corner: The Elusive Dream of Evangelical Unity* (Fearn, Ross-shire: Christian Focus Publications, 1999)

11. Faith and Joy

The Christian life is a life of constant, unhindered joy—or at least, so says the Apostle Paul: 'Rejoice in the Lord always; again I will say, Rejoice' (*Phil.* 4:4). According to Paul, joy is not to be an occasional feature in the believer's life; it is to be a constant reality, a daily, moment by moment reality. Does this seem a somewhat unreal expectation? Is Paul expecting too much? Is he even living in the real world, where disappointments, discouragements, and disasters can, and do, blast the believer's life? Is it not the height of spiritual escapism to think that Christians should always be rejoicing?

We can hardly, however, accuse Paul of engaging in spiritual escapism, or of suggesting that believers live trouble-free lives. For one thing, his own life was a catalogue of disappointments, discouragements, and disasters (read *2 Cor.* 11:23-29); and for another, he never tired of telling Christians that the life of faith was a life beset with trials, temptations, and persecutions (read *Acts* 14:21, 22; *2 Tim.* 3:10-12). Paul was no head-in-the-cloud Christian. He well knew, by bitter experience, the pains and sorrows of the believing life. And yet, he still writes, 'Rejoice in the Lord always'; and in case we don't quite take in the force of what he has said, he repeats himself, 'again I will say, Rejoice.'

Paul is well aware of how seemingly impossible his command (for that is what it is) will appear to us. But in no sense is Paul suggesting that Christians will always have the sunshine of God's love and goodness shining on their backs, making it easy for them to rejoice. What he is saying, however, is that in spite of all the troubles and discouragements and disasters that can, and do, overtake the child of God, he is still able to 'rejoice.' How can that be?

Look carefully at what Paul writes: 'Rejoice in the Lord.' The Christian is to rejoice always because his joy is pre-eminently located not in his circumstances, but in his Saviour — in the unchanging and unchangeable Lord Jesus Christ! Paul is not saying for one moment that believers should be walking around with a permanent grin, saying 'Praise the Lord!' every second sentence. For one thing, this is not the picture the Scriptures give us of our Lord Jesus, the proto-typical man of faith. Our Saviour knew the sore reality of disappointments and discouragements; he experienced the greatest weariness; he was 'despised and rejected by men'. Christians are able to 'Rejoice always', because our joy is in who our God and Saviour is and in what he has done for us; and nothing can change his love for us, or change the constancy of his faithful character. This means that no matter what befalls a Christian, he is still a child of God, a forgiven sinner, a heaven-bound saint, the most blessed being in the cosmos! If the Christian loses everything, he still has everything, for he cannot lose his Saviour, who is his great salvation (2 *Cor.* 6:10).

Martin Luther saw this and concluded his great Reformation hymn, 'A Mighty Fortress is Our God', with these words:

> Let goods and kindred go,
>   this mortal life also;
> The body they may kill:
>   God's truth abideth still;
> His kingdom is forever.

Paul is not saying that the Christian will always appear to be full of joy; but even through the bitterest of tears, the believing heart can rejoice in the Lord. Even in times of deepest and darkest perplexity, the child of God can rejoice, not because he can fully understand God's ways with him, but because he has a Saviour, who loved him and gave himself for him, and who loves him now and forever.

Christian joy can at times be 'out of this world' (*1 Pet.*1:8). At other times it may be covered by an avalanche of trials and discouragements. But can we not always rejoice, seeing that our Lord Jesus is God over all, blessed forever; that he, who bore our sin and shame, is seated on the throne of the universe; that one day we shall see him as he is, and be forever with him? Jesus is our cause for constant rejoicing.

12. Faith in the Dark

Sometimes Christians fall into the depths of utter despair. An extreme example would be Jeremiah, God's faithful prophet. We can hardly imagine the inner anguish that caused him to cry out, 'Cursed be the day on which I was born . . . Why did I come out from the womb to see toil and sorrow, and spend my days in shame?' (*Jer.* 20:14, 18). Jeremiah didn't end his days in shame, but at a particularly dark time in his life he was sure that he would. Many of us perhaps have little idea what it must be like to be in the depths of despair. It may be that temperamentally we are somewhat immune from such experiences, or are strangers to the spiritual battles that some of God's choicest servants are called to fight. What cannot be denied is that even the finest of Christians are exposed by their gracious and kindly Father to the darkest of experiences. Most remarkably, it was the Holy Spirit who led our Lord Jesus into the desert, where for forty days he was tempted by the devil.

Why is this? Why does our heavenly Father purpose such dark valleys for some of his dearly loved children? No doubt much could be said. One reason is because he loves his children and seeks their present and eternal good. For our Lord Jesus Christ, it was his exposure to the assaults of the evil one that prepared him for the ministry and mission that lay before him. The first

Adam failed and fell with all the advantages of God's presence and garden to sustain him; the last Adam triumphed and prevailed in a desert, with nothing but his naked trust in his Father and the support of the Holy Spirit to sustain him: 'Man shall not live by bread alone, but by every word that comes from the mouth of God' (*Matt.* 4:4).

Conformity to the Lord Jesus Christ will necessarily mean that we enter into the pattern of life that made him the Man he became: 'he learned obedience through what he suffered. And being made perfect, he became the source of eternal salvation to all who obey him' (*Heb.* 5:8, 9). The dark valleys are no less part of our heavenly Father's gracious purpose for his children, than are the sun-lit mountain tops. We would, of course, rather always be on the mountain top, but there are lessons and truths that can only be learnt in the dark valleys lovingly prepared by our heavenly Father. It is neither callousness nor indifference that causes him to lead us into the valley of the shadow of death; it is rather his unshakeable resolve to conform us to the likeness of his Son.

A second reason why the Lord allows his precious children to 'walk in the valley of the shadow of death', bereft of the sense of his loving presence, is highlighted by Paul in 2 Corinthians 1:8f. Paul and his companions' circumstances were so dire that he wrote, 'we despaired of life itself. Indeed, we felt we had received the sentence of death.' But the apostle goes on to say,

'But that was to make us rely not on ourselves but on God who raises the dead.' In the dark valley God seeks to stretch and deepen our trust in him. In his wise and ever gracious providence he removes all our felt comforts from us and says, 'In your darkness trust me and prove me to be your complete sufficiency.' There are experiences of the God of grace that can only be known in dark valleys.

In the Prophecy of Isaiah there is a remarkable verse that encapsulates the teaching of God's word for believers when all the lights go out. At a particularly dark period in Israel's history, God spoke to the nation through his prophet:

> Who among you fears the LORD and obeys the word of his servant? Let him who walks in the darkness and has no light trust in the name of the LORD and rely on his God (*Isa.* 50:10).

Those words, 'who has no light', are awesome and fearsome. No light! Not a glimmer, not a pin-prick, just unremitting darkness. Does it seem incredible to you that such could be the experience of an authentic Christian? We would be tempted to say to a professing believer whose life was consumed by darkness, 'Are you sure you have really repented and trusted alone in the Lord Jesus Christ as Lord and Saviour? Has God's Spirit really come to dwell within you?' And yet, here we find God's own people, who 'fear the Lord' and 'obey the word of his servant', being encouraged, by their Lord, in their overwhelming and all-consuming darkness, to 'trust in the name of the LORD'.

These words of Isaiah are surely the Old Testament equivalent of Paul's 'we live by faith and not by sight' (2 *Cor.* 5:7). Faith is not only the gospel instrument that unites us to Christ, it is also the grace that keeps us walking in the way of Christ.

It is almost impossible to know what it must be like to have no light. The sense of the absence of God's presence can be demoralizing and devastating. And yet, the Lord's counsel to his light-less children is this, 'Trust me!' In particular, 'Trust who I am' ('the name of the LORD'). This is the ultimate issue, it seems to me, in the life of faith; when faced with a choice, will we believe the testimony of our circumstances, or will we believe the character of the God who is love, and who loves his children with a love that 'spared not his only Son but gave him up for us all'?

The life of faith, believing in the Lord Jesus Christ, is subject, for many reasons, to difficulties, discouragements, oppositions, hardships, disappointments, and much worse. But it is also subject to 'joy that is inexpressible and filled with glory' (1 *Pet.*1:8). In all of faith's highs and lows the Lord calls us to trust him. Behind a 'frowning providence, he hides a smiling face'.[1] In our Saviour's darkest moment, when the darkness of

---

[1] From William Cowper's hymn, 'God moves in a mysterious way'.

the sun symbolised the darkness covering his soul, even then he cried, 'My God, my God . . .?' He had no light, but in his darkness (which of course was redemptively unique darkness), he trusted in *his* God.

Some who read this may even now be in the depths and even feel utterly out of your depth. Perhaps you are wondering what it will mean for you in practice to 'trust in the name of the LORD and rely on [your] God'? Remember, therefore, what our Lord Jesus did in his times of great need (and he had them):

First, he quoted the word of God to the enemy who had tracked him into the desert place. Our Saviour repelled the wicked suggestions and temptations of the devil by the truth of Holy Scripture (*Luke* 4:1-12). He had hidden God's word in his heart that he might not sin against his God. This is what we all must learn to do. Gather up the precious promises of God's word, not least this one, 'the blood of Jesus Christ, God's Son, cleanses us from every sin', and suck the goodness out of them.

Secondly, he cried out to his Father. In the Garden of Gethsemane and on the cross, our Lord Jesus cried out to the One who loved him, to whom he was precious beyond all words. This is what the Psalmist did (read *Psa.* 130) when he was in the depths, 'Out of the depths I cry to you, O LORD [the God of covenant faithfulness]! O Lord, hear my voice.'

The wonderful encouragement the Scriptures give us is that the Holy Spirit 'helps us in our weakness. For we do not know what to pray for as we ought, but the Spirit himself intercedes for us with groanings too deep for words' (*Rom.* 8:26). In our extremities, the Holy Spirit, our indwelling Comforter and Counsellor, bears us up and carries us on.

Perhaps the hardest thing to do when you are in the depths is to resist the pressure to look in and find something inside yourself to bring you comfort: my love for him is not dead; I still trust him; I feel some sorrow for my sin; or whatever. It is good that such things are there; but what if tomorrow you feel they are not there? Charitie Lees De Chenez was profoundly right when she wrote:

> When Satan tempts me to despair,
>   And tells me of the guilt within,
> Upwards I look, and see Him there
>   Who made an end of all my sin.[1]

Help and hope are not found within, but without, in the finished work and unchanging love of our Great High Priest Jesus Christ—who is afflicted in all our afflictions.

Be of good cheer, dear Christian. The dark valleys will not last forever. One day they will all be swallowed up in the mountain-top glory of God's nearer presence. Then all our blues will be banished into eternal oblivion. He who promised is faithful.

---

[1] From the hymn, 'Before the throne of God above'.

13. Faith's Great Delight

Reading the *Letters of Samuel Rutherford* is to enter a world where love to the Lord Jesus Christ is the absorbing preoccupation. Writing to a lady parishioner in 1637, he said,

> Christ is a well of life; but who knoweth how deep it is to the bottom? . . . And oh, what a fair one, what an only one, what an excellent, lovely, ravishing one is Jesus.[1]

Such language, and, vastly more importantly, such heart affection, appears remote, perhaps even embarrassing, to many Christians today. Neither our language about the Saviour, nor our discoursing on the Saviour, gives the impression that he is the love of our lives, the One we cherish and adore above life itself. Why are we such strangers to the unembarrassed ardour that so marked Rutherford's (and that of multitudes of other Christians past and present), relationship with the Lord Jesus?

One answer that is sometimes given is that our temperaments are somewhat culturally conditioned and cannot be expected to be 'fulsome' and 'uninhibited': we are English or Scottish after all! We don't wear our hearts on our sleeves! Aside from the fact that Rutherford was as Scottish as you can get, this answer

[1] Rutherford, *Letters*, p. 446.

is but a sad excuse. There is little doubt that the Lord has given his world a wonderful cultural and temperamental diversity. But according to our Lord Jesus, the extravagance of our love to him is not conditioned by geography, race, or temperament, but by our grasp of his grace to us in the gospel.

In his Gospel Luke recounts for us in the greatest detail, the anointing of the Lord Jesus by 'a woman of the city, who was a sinner' (*Luke* 7:36-50). As the woman lavishes her love on the Saviour, Simon, Jesus' host, says to himself, 'If this man were a prophet, he would have known who and what sort of woman this is who is touching him, for she is a sinner' (verse 39). Jesus' response takes us to the heart of the matter. As he concludes his searching exposure of Simon's heart, he says, 'Therefore I tell you, her sins, which are many, are forgiven—for she loved much. But he who is forgiven little, loves little' (verse 47). Consider what our Lord is saying to us. The reason why the sinful woman lavished her affections so openly and extravagantly on him was because she had a deep sense of the wonder of the forgiveness of her sins. The reason we love our Saviour so haltingly and so mutedly is because we have lost the sense of the wonder and blessedness and glory of the forgiveness of our sins.

There can be no doubting that personal love to Christ grows in the fertile soil of personal indebtedness to God for his undeserved mercy to hell-deserving sinners. The Apostle John says the same thing: 'This is love: not that we loved God, but that he loved us and sent his Son as a propitiation for our sins.' Love to Christ, love that is not mere emotion, comes to birth and is nourished in the soil of God's gracious, sovereign, unfathomable, inexplicable love to guilty, judgment-deserving rebels. It is as we 'survey the wondrous cross on which the Prince of glory died' that we begin to love the Saviour—and continue to love him. There are no shortcuts. No easy to follow steps. No once-for-all 'love-sealing' experiences. No! Our Lord wants our love to him ever to be impregnated with the daily wonder and freshness of his love to us.

So, ponder Calvary. And ponder it again. And ponder it again—until, as the hymn puts it,

> Yes, teach me, till there gloweth
> In this cold heart of mine
> Some feeble, pale reflection
> Of that pure love of Thine.[1]

The Scriptures, however, have something else of vital importance to say to us on this matter. Learning to love the Saviour is not the private preserve of the Christian. While we so often think in personal, atomistic categories, the Scriptures think in corporate and covenantal categories. Let me illustrate: as he concludes his prayer for the church in Ephesus, Paul prays, 'And I pray that you, being rooted and established in love, may have

[1] From Lucy Ann Bennett's hymn, 'O teach me what it meaneth'.

power, *together with all the saints,* to grasp how wide and long and high and deep is the love of Christ, and to know this love that surpasses knowledge . . .' (*Eph.* 3:20). 'Together with all the saints'! Paul does not pray that they will love Christ better, but that *together* they will know Christ's love for them better! The focus is on Christ's love for his church, not the church's love for him—because, it's as we grasp the illimitable dimensions of his love for us, that we will grow in our love for him. And we are to do this 'together'. The church, the body of Christ, his precious bride, is a unity. Of course every individual Christian has a personal relationship with the Lord. But more importantly and fundamentally, the Lord relates to his people as his church. It is in corporate fellowship 'with all the saints', and not on our 'ownsome', that we are brought to know 'how wide and long and high and deep is the love of Christ'. If nothing else, this is a plea that we prize and cherish the church of Christ; that we commit ourselves to its worship, service, witness, and fellowship; that we mortify the temptation (for temptation it is) practically to exalt ourselves above the body of Christ and pursue the spiritual life in heart isolation from 'all the saints'.

The plaintive words of William Cowper are rarely out of my mind. I think he says what every truly Christian heart feels:

> Lord, it is my chief complaint
> That my love is weak and faint;

Yet I love Thee, and adore;
O for grace to love Thee more![1]

How then can we begin to love our Saviour better? How can we love him more ardently, more extravagantly, less self-consciously? There are no slick formulae, no out-of-this-world experiences to cultivate, simply this: Consider Jesus! Contemplate Calvary! Make the time and take the time to meditate on God's amazing grace to hell-deserving sinners. There is no substitute for loving Christ. Let Rutherford have the last word:

> Give Christ your virgin love: you cannot put your love and heart into a better hand. Oh! If ye knew him, and saw his beauty, your love, your liking, your heart, your desires would close with him and cleave to him . . . O fair sun, and fair moon, and fair stars, and fair flowers, and fair roses, and fair lilies, and fair creatures, but O ten thousand times fairer Lord Jesus.[2]

[1] From the hymn, 'Hark, my soul! it is the Lord'.
[2] Rutherford, *Letters,* p. 398.

14. *The Sweet Words that Nourish Faith*

One of the most staggering verses in the Bible is surely Romans 8:28; 'And we know that in all things God works for the good of those who love him, who are the called according to his purpose.' What is so breathtaking here is the scope of Paul's conviction, 'in *all* things', and the unbounded assurance of his conviction, 'we *know*'. There is nothing tentative about his conviction; he declares it as an unassailable, incontrovertible Christian given. But how can Paul be so sure? Does he really mean 'in all things'? Can he really mean 'in all things'? Is it really true that God is able to work my darkest experiences, my sorest struggles and even my sins, for my good and his glory? By the immediate and infallible inspiration of the Holy Spirit, so the apostle asserts!

In no sense is Paul engaging in mere wishful thinking; nor is he exercising the power of positive thinking! Paul is writing personally and experimentally. He has proven in his own experience that what he says is so. But more foundationally, Paul is writing theologically. 'We know that in all things . . . For . . .' In the following verses, the apostle explains how he is so sure that 'in all things God is at work for the good of those who love him.' The panorama of his argument is quite astonishing: he tells us that God has an invincible purpose, a purpose that begins with him lovingly predestinating a people to be conformed to the likeness of his Son, and ends with him glorifying every single one of those people. Here is pristine pastoralia! In an age of pseudo-spiritual psychotherapy, we need more than ever to recover God's principal means of breathing hope and encouragement into the hard-pressed and at times demoralised lives of his children—the application of doctrine to life!

It is one of the most significant growth points in the Christian life when it dawns upon us that God's truth is not simply for believing and confessing, but also for living! God's principal means of establishing and reassuring his children is to ground us in his truth, to infect our minds and hearts with doctrines, precepts, and promises that rescue us from the debilitating grip of circumstances and help us to see our lives 'theologically'. This is practical Christianity.

Of course, what Paul asserts in this verse has been used as an excuse for some professing Christians to go on sinning, assuming that God will always be there to pick up the pieces and put everything right. To think like that, however, is to betray yourself as a yet godless wretch in need of the saving, life-transforming grace of God. That said, these are sweet words to God's children. You know the struggles and trials you have gone through, and are perhaps presently going through. You know only too well those failures that daily condemn you and haunt you. You know the dark providences that our heavenly Father mysteriously on occasion brings into his dear children's lives: 'And we know that in all things God works for the good of those who love him . . .' He does this sovereignly, mysteriously, universally, purposefully, and ultimately gloriously. Far from being an encouragement for a Christian to live as he pleases, this glorious truth always causes the true Christian to worship and glory in such a gracious and good God, and to seek in all things to please him.

The Puritan John Flavel wrote, 'Some providences are like the Hebrew alphabet, they are best read backwards.' It will not be until we arrive in Immanuel's Land, that we will see the perfection of our God's graciously sovereign dealings with us. Until then we have his immutable promise, 'that in all things' he is working 'for the good of those who love him, who are the called according to his purpose'. Pastoral ministry may not end here, but it always begins here. That is simply to say, that God in Christ is our greatest comfort.

15. *The Aroma of Faith*

I recently read in James Denney's *Commentary on 2 Corinthians* these words:

> . . . as Paul moved through the world, all who had eyes to see saw in him not only the power but the

sweetness of God's redeeming love. The mighty Victor made manifest through him, not only His might, but His charm, not only His greatness, but His grace.

These are surely striking words. Denney is reflecting on the phrase in 2 Corinthians 2:14, where Paul speaks of God, through his saved people, spreading 'everywhere the fragrance of the knowledge of him'. Just as the sweet smell of burning incense filled Rome when a victorious general returned from battle, so, says Paul, the triumph and truth of the crucified Christ is proclaimed fragrantly by the lips and lives of Christ's captive people.

That Paul should speak of the 'fragrance' of the knowledge of Christ is both deeply striking and profoundly searching. We are accustomed, and rightly so, to think of the profound importance of gospel truth being proclaimed *accurately*. Truth is at a discount in our so-called post-modern world. Christians need more than ever today to assert, and to do so passionately, the objective, unassailable truth of God's revelation in Jesus Christ. But when we proclaim the gospel, and when we live out the gospel (the gospel inevitably issues in a transformed, that is commandment-obedient, life), do we always succeed in manifesting it *fragrantly*? Or, is the truth that the gospel's fragrance, sweetness, winsomeness, charm and attractiveness, is the very thing that is most easily and often missing?

We all surely have known the compelling appeal and power of a sermon through a life that has radiated the 'fragrance of the knowledge of Christ'. The truth has come to us, not coldly or clinically, but clothed in the grace of our Lord Jesus Christ. We have heard the dark and solemn truths of sin and righteousness and judgment; but we heard them come from lives that expressed the fragrance of the 'Rose of Sharon'. The truth was clothed with grace and winsomeness.

Why is it then, that Reformed Christians, Calvinists if you will, are so often accused of being cold and clinical, 'the frozen chosen'? The answer could well be, of course, that our fellow Christians are simply reacting against our unyielding commitment to let God be God, and to reverence him who is a 'consuming fire'. But the answer could also be that we have been guilty at times of divorcing the truth of Christ from union with Christ. Let me explain. In 2 Corinthians 2:15 Paul speaks of God leading 'us in triumphal procession in Christ and through us' spreading 'everywhere the fragrance of the knowledge of him'. Everything in the Christian life flows from our union with the Lord Jesus Christ. All the saving and sanctifying blessings we enjoy in the gospel come to us in union with Christ. He is the vine, we are the branches. The sap of his life, by the Holy Spirit, flows through the believer's life. This is why Paul can write of the 'fruit of the Spirit' (*Gal.* 5:22, 23), and give us a description of the life of the Saviour, with all its grace, winsomeness, and charm. If gospel truth is not clothed with the grace of our Lord Jesus Christ, is it really 'gospel' ('good news') truth?

This in no sense means that gospel truth will never be stern or searchingly humbling. But it does mean that we will speak it and live it as men and women humbled by its grace, filled with its joy, thrilled by its possibilities, harnessed to the One who is 'full of grace and truth'.

James Denney was not over-stating the point when he wrote:

> We miss what is most characteristic in the knowledge of God if we miss this. We leave out that very element in the Evangel which makes it evangelic, and gives it its power to subdue and enchain the souls of men.

How 'fragrantly' do our lives and our sermons commend the Saviour, 'the Rose of Sharon'.

16. *Faith's Great Sorrow*

George Swinnock (a mid-seventeenth century Puritan) wrote some words that remarkably describe twenty-first century evangelical Christianity:

> We take the size of sin too low, and short, and wrong, when we measure it by the wrong it doth to ourselves, or our families, or our neighbours, or the nation wherein we live; indeed, herein somewhat of its evil and mischief doth appear; but to take its full

length and proportion, we must consider the wrong
it doth to this great, this glorious, this incomparable God. Sin is incomparably malignant, because
the God principally injured by it is incomparably
excellent.[1]

Swinnock, of course, is saying no more than the Bible
itself says. The ultimate tragedy of sin is not that it spoils
my life, disrupts my relationships, scars my world, but
that it dishonours, defies, and disgraces my God.

This is a truth, a most basic and elementary truth,
that I fear our present generation of Christians has all
but lost sight of. Sin, if it is mentioned at all, is conceived
of almost wholly in self-referential terms. It is described
in terms of its 'psychological pains and its relational
disruptions'. And truly sin does produce deep psychological pains and relational disruptions. The heart and
horror of sin, however, is not its effect on me, but its
effect on God, 'the incomparably excellent' God. This is
remarkably highlighted in Psalm 51:4. King David has
been deeply convicted of his sin in taking Bathsheba, the
wife of Uriah. He has compounded his sin by conspiring
to have Uriah murdered. And yet, when he comes to
cry to God for mercy, David prays, 'Against you, you
only, have I sinned and done what is evil in your sight.'
David is not denying his sin against Bathsheba, Uriah,
his own family, God's church. He is, however, telling

[1] George Swinnock, *Works of George Swinnock* (Edinburgh:
Banner of Truth, 1992), 4:456.

himself, and us, that the true horror of sin is that it is against God. Sin's ultimate tragedy can only be defined theologically, not psychologically or relationally.

This is a truth the evangelical church needs to become re-acquainted with in our day. We live in a self-referential culture. The church, rightly, wants to minister the gospel of God's grace and love into this culture. The ever-present danger facing us, however, is that we contour the Bible's teaching on sin to suit the felt needs of this culture. This is a problem many Christians have with the *Alpha Course*. The initial concern of *Alpha* was laudable: How can we best reach the un-churched pagans in our society with the good news of the Lord Jesus Christ? I, for one, deeply admire that desire, and am rebuked by it. But when you look carefully at the *Alpha Course*, it basically seeks to present sin almost solely as a psychological, personal, and social disrupter. And sin is such a disrupter. It is the root of all the evils in this world, personal and global. But until men and women are helped to see that the horror of sin is that it is against God, and makes you his enemy (*Rom.* 5:10), Jesus Christ will never be seen for what he most essentially is, the One sent from God, and by God, to reconcile us to God, deliver us from the coming wrath, and fit us for eternal fellowship with God. The root of all our ills is our sin-ruptured relationship with the living God.

Many of the great theologians of the Christian church have called sin '*Deicidium*', literally 'God murder'! Is that how you and I think of sin? We can so easily lose the felt sense, if not the theological fact, of the sinfulness of sin. If we do, we end up talking about sin in ways that sit easily with our culture. And when we speak of sin only in self-referential and therapeutic terms, moral responsibility diminishes proportionately. Is there not an obvious connection between the loss of the theological dimension of sin and the moral collapse at the heart of professing evangelicalism?

Where does all this leave us? Not simply parroting what the Puritans preached four centuries ago. They were men of their times; they understood the times they lived in—and so must we understand our own times. We must labour to speak relevantly into this culture. Paul's address in Athens (*Acts* 17) is perhaps a model for us in many ways. We need to speak to people where they are, not where we would like them to be. We need to be less concerned with 'success' and more concerned with 'faithfulness'. We need to cultivate Paul's confidence: 'we have renounced disgraceful, underhanded ways. We refuse to practise cunning or to tamper with God's word, but by open statement of the truth we would commend ourselves to everyone's conscience in the sight of God' (2 *Cor.* 4:2). One of our great challenges is to commend the gospel relevantly without becoming gimmicky. This is easier said than done; but do it we must.

Where then do we start? With sin? No; with God! Let me end, as I began, with some words from George Swinnock:

should this God of glory appear to thee . . . and show thee a glimpse of his excellent glory . . . should he discover to thee but a little of that greatness which the heavens and heaven of heavens cannot contain . . . of those perfections that know no bounds . . . what wouldst thou then think of sin?

If we are to see sin for what it truly is, we must first come to see God as he truly is. And so Thomas Goodwin wrote, 'if thou wouldst see what sin is, go to mount Calvary'[1]—because there, we see God as he most truly is. The cross of Christ is the glory and the measure of everything. It is in the searing light of the sin-bearing, substitutionary death of Christ, that we begin to see the heart and horror of sin. What must the holy God of heaven think of sin, our rebellion against him and his holy law, if it took nothing less than the blood-shedding of his own Son to rescue us from its condemning guilt and imprisoning power? Grasping even a little the exceeding sinfulness of sin will magnify the Saviour's love and grace in your eyes.

[1] Thomas Goodwin, *Works of Thomas Goodwin* (Edinburgh: Nichol, 1863), 5:287.

17. The Humble Wisdom of Faith

Henry Ford famously stated 'History is bunk!' Far from being 'bunk', however, history is the unfolding of God's redemptive purposes, it bears the imprint of his grace and judgments, and is intended to awaken us to eternal realities. This conviction confronts us every time we open God's word. Again and again, the biblical writers refer to God's dealings in history to impress on God's people the vast importance of taking their God seriously. 'Remember Lot's wife', our Lord Jesus counselled his disciples.

It was with this conviction that in 1857, J. C. Ryle wrote a little tract entitled *The Finger of God*. He was quoting, of course, the words of Pharaoh's magicians as they saw their land afflicted by yet another plague. Ryle explains at the outset of his tract what it was that spurred him to write:

> There is an evil among us that demands our serious attention. It forces itself on our notice, whether we like it or not. It has seized the nation by the throat, and will have a hearing. That evil is THE FOOT AND MOUTH EPIDEMIC.

Ryle goes on to insist that the epidemic had been sent from God 'as a special national chastisement . . . because of our special national sins.' In other words, Ryle was urging the nation to recognise 'the finger of God' in the agricultural calamity that was now afflicting it. God judges nations. God does not stand idly by while nations live heedless of his general and special revelation—he is a righteous and just God.

Who of us would deny the national sins that presently scar our nation? Ryle lists seven sins that blighted national life in his day; covetousness, luxury and the love of pleasure, neglect of the Lord's day, drunkenness, contempt of the seventh commandment (adultery), a growing tendency to look favourably on the Roman Catholic Church, scepticism and infidelity. As the nation continues its headlong plunge into ruin, we could add to Ryle's list.

The tragedy, of course, is that historically we have been a vastly privileged nation. Our nation is not a stranger to gospel truth. The Reformation was a great mercy from God. But we have squandered our inheritance. We are much like the prodigal son; we are in the far country, eating pigswill, and in desperate need of coming to our senses. Is this not then how we should view the calamities that occasionally overtake our nation? Should we not see them as 'severe mercies', sore providences sent by a just, but merciful God, to awaken us to the folly of sin? It is an indelibly engraved truth that 'Righteousness exalts a nation', and 'sin is a reproach to any people' (*Prov.* 14:34). If we sow the wind, we inevitably reap the whirlwind. It is because the Lord has the eternal good of sinners at heart that he sends his judgments as awakening providences. It was C. S. Lewis who wrote, 'God whispers to us in our pleasures, speaks in our conscience, but shouts in our pains: it is His megaphone to rouse a deaf world.'

What then are we to do? We should see sore providences for what they are, 'severe mercies'. We should humble ourselves under God's almighty hand, in order that he might lift us up in due time. This was Ryle's counsel to the people of his own day; but he went on to write, 'Alas, we are a proud and conceited nation . . . We are sadly blind to our many faults and sins.' Is that not precisely how it is with us today? More than ever we need to pray to the One who tells us he is 'merciful and gracious', and 'slow to anger', who hears and answers prayer.

On the day of Jesus Christ, many will bless God for his 'severe mercies'. Yes, his judgments are sore and humbling; but he 'takes no pleasure in the death of the wicked', he would rather, much rather, that we turn to him and live (*Ezek.* 33:11). This is what the cross shouts out to us. There are no lengths to which God will not go, and has not gone, to save us from a lost and ruined eternity. May the Lord graciously give us the wisdom to see his 'finger' at work, and the grace to repent of our national and personal sins.

18. Loving One Another:
the Family Character of Faith

When Augustine found himself in controversy with fellow believers, he remarked on more than one occasion to his friend Alypius, 'Remember, we are washed in the same blood.' The great church father was not down playing the importance of doctrine. Rather, he was highlighting the foundational truth that, whatever their differences, believers are one in Christ. There is, as Paul reminds the Christians in Ephesus, but 'one Lord, one faith, one baptism' (*Eph.* 4:5).

Why mention this? For this reason: It is only too easy to so prize accurate doctrine that we lose sight of our unity in Christ with all believers everywhere. I am very conscious that this is easy to say and harder to put into practice. We, at least I, instinctively think in terms of theological, even denominational, distinctives. We become suspicious of professing Christians who are not 'one of us' (read *Mark* 9:38-41). I have been wonderfully privileged to have been embraced by the Reformed Faith. Like many of you, I am persuaded it is the most accurate and enriching explication of the teaching of God's holy word. But precisely here lies a danger: the Reformed Faith is not the Christian Faith — unless you believe that everyone who is not a Calvinistic

Presbyterian is not a Christian at all! Sadly, some give the impression (and more than the impression) that if you are not wholly committed to the *Westminster Confession of Faith*, you are deeply suspect. I would guess that an incipient sectarianism is more widespread in our circles than we would like to admit. In some places there is almost the mentality that says, The smaller your church is, the purer and more orthodox it must be. How can we counter this profoundly unbiblical and un-Christian attitude?

John Calvin has a wonderful passage in Book 4.10.30 of his *Institutes of the Christian Religion*, that points us in a wholesome and deeply Christian direction for an answer. While acknowledging that in the ordering of our worship 'we ought not to charge into innovation rashly, suddenly', he continued, 'it will be fitting (as the advantage of the church will require) to change and abrogate traditional practices and to establish new ones'. No doubt conscious that what he has just written could be misunderstood, Calvin concludes, 'But love will best judge what may hurt or edify; and if we let love be our guide, all will be safe.' Calvin is acknowledging that Christians will not always see things the same way or do things the same way. When we differ, 'let love be our guide and all will be safe'. How you react and respond to those words will say a lot about you.

Of course they are 'dangerous' words. Often Christians have used 'love' as a pretext for not publicly opposing error in the church and for glossing over doctrinal aberrations. But, and it is a big 'but', didn't our Lord Jesus say, 'By this all people will know that you are my disciples, if you love one another' (*John* 13:35)? Our Saviour was not advocating that his disciples ignore differences, turn a benign eye to heresy, and embrace everyone who says they are a Christian. He surely, however, was saying that his disciples, imitating him, were to embrace everyone born again of his Spirit and loved by his Father. If a Christian is someone who trusts in Christ alone for salvation (*John* 3:16; 3:36; *Acts* 16:31, etc.), then we are duty bound to treat as brothers and sisters all who have been 'brothered' by Christ—'we are washed in the same blood'.

This is our Christian starting point. Of course we will seek to challenge our less than Reformed brothers and sisters to embrace the riches of God's sovereign grace in the gospel. Of course, if you are anything like me, you will want to help and challenge fellow believers to see the rich biblical truth of God's covenant grace to families. But our starting point will always be, 'These are my people; we have been washed in the same blood, sanctified by the same Spirit, and loved by the same Father.' Such a view may strike you as uncommonly naïve. Perhaps. However, it is the naïveté of God's word. It makes the Christian life less clinical and more 'messy' and certainly more demanding. But it also expresses something of the Father's love for all his children.

I have no easy solutions. But our Saviour prayed for the unity of his family (*John* 17:20ff.). If he prayed for it, we should labour to realise it. If it was worth his blood, it is worthy of our effort. 'Be imitators of God, therefore, as dearly loved children and live a life of love, just as Christ loved us and gave himself up for us as a fragrant offering and sacrifice to God' (*Eph.* 5:1, 2).

19. *Where Faith Always Looks*

I have never been in the habit of making New Year resolutions. They have always seemed somewhat artificial. Why wait till a new year dawns before making a resolution? Recently, however, I broke the habit of a lifetime and made a resolution. Before I share it with you, allow me to explain how I came to make it.

I had been reading through the Letter to the Hebrews. It had, as ever, been a fascinating, sobering, and richly encouraging read. The letter, as you will know, was written to Hebrew Christians who had become influenced by false teaching and were under pressure to give up on Christ and return to Judaism. They had 'become dull of hearing' (*Heb.* 5:11). They no longer listened to God's word in Christ as they once had. They had not always been in this sad (and perilous) spiritual state. Slowly but surely, however, they had become spiritually deaf to God's word. What had caused this? Why had they become near insensible to God's truth? The answer given in Hebrews is seen in three exhortations: 'holy brothers who share in a heavenly calling, consider Jesus . . . looking to Jesus the founder and perfecter of the faith . . . Consider him' (*Heb.* 3:1; 12:2; 12:3). Three times the writer encourages his spiritually debilitated readers to 'fix their eyes [thoughts] on Jesus'. In other words, they were in this sad spiritual condition because they had taken their eyes off their Saviour. Their great need was to re-focus their lives in Christ, to consider him, to ponder anew the grace of the Lord Jesus Christ.

Somehow they had allowed the pressures of life, and they were experiencing great pressures (read *Heb.* 10:32ff.; 13:3), to de-centre Jesus in their lives. He was no longer the chief object of their faith and the first call upon their love. In many respects the whole of the letter is a sustained appeal for these embattled believers to see just how great their Saviour is: superior to all God's angels; superior to great Moses; superior to Aaron and the priesthood; he is the One who is faithful over God's house 'as a Son' (*Heb.* 3:6); he is the One who 'has appeared once for all at the end of the ages to put away sin by the sacrifice of himself' (*Heb.* 9:26); he is the One who 'always lives to make intercession' for God's children (*Heb.* 7:25); and he is the One who is not ashamed to call us his brothers (*Heb.* 2:11).

They were in danger of drifting away from the gospel because they had stopped 'considering him'. They had 'become dull of hearing' God's word because they had become less preoccupied with God's Son.

It was with this in my mind that I resolved, God helping me, more deliberately to 'consider him' in this coming year. I know that this should be the daily resolve of every Christian. But I felt in myself the need to make that resolve more deliberate.

I want, then, to encourage you to resolve, God helping you, to 'consider him'. Can you think of a better resolution? Are you satisfied that you 'consider him' as purposefully and as seriously as you should? Is it not true for you as it always has been for me, that when your heart grows cold and you begin to wander, it is ALWAYS because you have not been fixing your thoughts and centring your hearts in your blessed Saviour?

Consider him! The Great High Priest who represents you and cares for you and prays for you at the Father's right hand; the King who lovingly and tenderly rules you; the Prophet who is himself God's last and best word to a fallen, sinful world. The old chorus may not score high in poetry, but its theology is impeccable:

> Turn your eyes upon Jesus,
>   Look full in His wonderful face,
> And the things of earth will grow strangely dim,
>   In the light of His glory and grace.[1]

[1] From Helen H. Lemmel's hymn, 'O soul, are you weary and troubled?'

20. *Faith at Work*

John Bunyan's justly famous words are a helpful starting point for a brief comment on 'prayer': 'You can do more than pray after you have prayed, but you cannot do more than pray until you have prayed.' Bunyan is reminding us of the priority prayer is to have in the Christian life. Far from being peripheral and supplemental, prayer is central and fundamental. It truly is 'the Christian's vital breath.'

In his wonderful exposition on prayer in Book 3 of his *Institutes*, Calvin tells us it is by prayer 'that we reach those riches which are laid up for us with the Heavenly Father' (3.20.2). He continues, 'So true is it that we dig up by prayer the treasures that were pointed out by the Lord's gospel, and which our faith has gazed upon' (3.20.2). The picture Calvin paints of prayer 'digging up' the rich treasures of the gospel is surely instructive. We know that in our Lord Jesus Christ are to be found 'all the treasures of wisdom and knowledge' (*Col.* 2:3). But how are we to enjoy those riches? Surely the answer is, digging them up by believing prayer. We know that God is 'the master and bestower of all good things' and that he invites us to ask him to bless us with those good things. Didn't our Lord Jesus assure us; 'If you then, who are evil, know how to give good gifts to your children, how much more will your Father who is in heaven give good things to those who ask him' (*Matt.* 7:11).

This must surely be the greatest of all encouragements for a Christian to pray. Our heavenly Father delights to bless his children with his good gifts, that is, with the knowledge and experience of his love, presence, support, forgiveness, gentleness, and patient forbearance. But, he ministers his giving through our asking—'to those who ask him'.

And yet, even with such a wonderful encouragement, how slow we are to pray. Do you not often marvel at how sluggishly you pray? Are you not humbled by your reluctance to 'dig up' in prayer the treasures that are yours in Christ?

There are, perhaps, three main reasons why we struggle in prayer.

First, we give in to our often weary and care-distracted minds. Even when the spirit is willing, the flesh can be weak.

Second, Satan is an ever-present prayer-opposer. He hates to see God's children pray and will conjure up every distraction to divert you from prayer. The hymn-writer expresses this well,

> Satan trembles when he sees
> The weakest saint upon his knees.

Third, we fail to appreciate how ready our heavenly Father is to help us and bless us. He is the best of all fathers. He is the Father whose love for us is out of this world (*1 John* 3:1). He is a Father who remembers our frame and never forgets that we are dust (*Psa.* 103:12, 13).

The apostles resolved to give themselves 'to prayer and to the ministry of the word' (*Acts* 6:4). Paul pleaded, 'Pray for me'. James wrote, 'You do not have, because you do not ask' (*James* 4:2). As he prepared his disciples for his going to the Father, Jesus gave them the most wonderful of encouragements: 'If you abide in me, and my words abide in you, ask whatever you wish, and it will be done for you. By this my Father is glorified, that you bear much fruit and so prove to be my disciples' (*John* 15:7, 8). This is surely one of the most remarkable and extravagant promises in the Bible. Significantly, Jesus locates the fruitfulness of prayer in himself: 'If you abide in me, and my words abide in you. . .' There is an inherent condition to fruitful prayer. Jesus' extravagant promise is to those disciples who keep up close communion with himself and who allow every facet of their lives to be shaped and styled by his words. In this way the mind of Christ becomes our mind and so we shall ask and desire only that which accords with his mind and purpose and directed to his and the Father's glory.

Many years ago when I was a young Christian, my then minister, George Philip, quoted words I have never forgotten: 'Prayer is evangelism shorn of all its carnal attraction.' What do you think of that? This is where the battle is won or lost.

The last word belongs to the Psalmist: 'Trust him at all times, O people; pour out your hearts to him, for God is our refuge' (*Psa.* 62:8).

21. *What Faith Sees*

The Book of Esther is vastly encouraging and re-assuring. Nowhere is God's name mentioned, but his presence is everywhere evident. Simply reading through Esther confronts you, at every turn, with the palpable truth of God's sovereign providence: unseen, and unknown at least to King Ahasuerus and his Prime Minister Haman, the covenant Lord worked out 'all things according to the counsel of his will' (*Eph.* 1:11), for his own glory, and the preservation and good of his people.

What is so striking about the story of Esther is the sheer ordinariness and unobtrusiveness of God's providential workings. We see it perhaps most starkly in the 'international beauty contest' that decides who will be the next queen of Persia. We are told that Esther 'was lovely in form and features', and it was this beauty that first brought her to the attention of the palace officials. We are not to imagine that some happy accident of genetic configuration accounted for Esther's 'form and features': all she was, she was by the sovereign providence of God. It was God's decree which set her in her family line, gave her the parents who conceived her and shared their genes with her. How she looked, and the fact she was a stunning beauty, was due to God's providence. Even in the tackiness of a beauty contest (and few things are more tacky and pathetic than beauty contests), the covenant Lord was ordering events and controlling who would be chosen.

The point that the writer is skilfully, in an understated way, pressing upon us, is that even in such a worldly arena of sinful male chauvinism, God was at work, fulfilling his purposes and preserving his people.

There is a massive truth here for us to take to heart. Frederick William Faber put it well in his great hymn 'Workmen of God':

> Thrice blest is he to whom is giv'n
> The instinct that can tell
> That God is on the field, when He
> Is most invisible.

In every arena of life, even in the tacky arenas of wanton worldliness and political intrigue, our covenant Lord is providentially ordering events to secure his glory and the building of his church in the world. Christians need never despair, no matter the situation or circumstances. If our God can overrule a beauty contest for his people's good, there is no event he cannot bend to accomplish his sovereign will. The God of Israel was accomplishing his purposes, and everyone looking on, only saw men ogling at beautiful women. God not only uses the wrath of man to praise him, he uses all their pathetic schemes to advance his sovereign will, while never for one moment becoming contaminated by their wickedness.

When the Psalmist wrote 'My times are in your hand' (*Psa.* 31:15), he was encouraging his soul. As you look out on your particular circumstances and are at times tempted to despair, remember who your God is: the God who rules nations, presidents, prime ministers, and beauty contests. All you are—physically, temperamentally, intellectually—you are by God's decree. He providentially ordains and orders all your ways and the ways of all men and women everywhere. For the child of God, this is not first a conundrum to solve, it is a pillow to lie on! You may never end up in a beauty contest, but whatever your circumstances, it is not mere men who are 'calling the shots'; it is your covenant Lord who is shaping events and pursuing his purposes. This is why Faber wrote,

> Thrice blest is he to whom is giv'n
> The instinct that can tell
> That God is on the field, when He
> Is most invisible.

He is never off the field, even when the field is a tacky beauty contest. Our God reigns: that is why the peoples should tremble (*Psa.* 99:1).

22. *Faith's Highest Privilege*

The highest privilege a Christian can enjoy this side of eternity is fellowship or communion with God. John holds out the prospect of communion with God as the characteristic mark of the Christian fellowship: 'that which we have seen and heard we proclaim also to you, so that you too may have fellowship [communion] with us; and indeed our fellowship [communion] is with the Father and with his Son Jesus Christ' (1 John 1:3).

We all know this. But don't we also know (to our great shame) how intermittent and lukewarm and self-regarding is our communion with God? We know only too well how weakly and poorly we give to our Father and our Saviour those 'returns of love' that they seek from all their people. We (if you are anything like me) are much like the man John Owen wrote about: 'I cannot find my heart making returns of love unto God. Could I find my soul set upon Him, I could then believe His soul delighted in me.'[1] In our communion with God we are so prone to look first into our own hearts to see what love to Christ is there. In doing so we have fallen into the trap of 'anthropocentrism', that is we make ourselves the centre of the spiritual life, and view our communion with God through the cracked and skewed lens of our own hearts.

[1] Owen, *Works*, 2:37.

Owen responds vigorously to this 'anthropocentrism'. He writes,

> This is the most preposterous course that thy thoughts can pitch upon . . . 'Herein is love', saith the Holy Ghost, 'not that we loved God, but that he loved us' first . . . Now thou wouldst invert this order, and say, 'Herein is love, not that God loved me, but that I loved him first' . . . This is a course of flesh's finding out that will never bring glory to God, nor peace to thy own soul. Lay down then thy reasonings, take up the love of the Father upon a pure act of believing, and that will open up thy soul to let it out unto the Lord in the communion of love.[1]

Do Owen's words strike a chord with you?

How easily we can slide into a self-centred view of the life of faith. Almost before we know it, we are looking in, when we should be looking out and up. This is perhaps the most striking feature of Owen's wonderful treatise on *Communion with God*. It is so radically theocentric. This is the note that Owen wants to sound in our minds and hearts. In a deeply moving passage, he writes, 'Thoughts of communion with the saints were the joy of his [Christ's] heart from eternity.' Is this not the most reassuring, consoling and humbling of thoughts? Does such a thought not put a sword into the man-centredness that so afflicts the Christian church today? The centre of

[1] Owen, *Works*, 2:37

gravity in the believing life is not my love for him, but his great love for me. Grasping this would do more than anything else to rid the church of the self-absorption that mars its life, witness, and worship.

It was this 'God-centred communion' which prepared Owen for death. The day before he died, he dictated a last letter to a friend: 'I am going to him whom my soul hath loved, or rather who hath loved me with an everlasting love; which is the whole ground of all my consolation.'[1] Right to the last, Owen was looking out to God in Christ. What comforted him in life, consoled him in death — he was loved with an everlasting love.

Often we think that if only we grasped the 'deep things' of the gospel, our spiritual lives would deepen and flourish. The truth is, however, that our greatest need is always to grasp, and be grasped by, 'gospel basics', and nothing is more basic than grasping that in Christ I am loved, dearly loved, with an everlasting love.

Let me leave you with one last gem from Owen. He assures us that Christ's 'heart is glad in [his people] without sorrow'. In saying this, Owen is echoing Zephaniah 3:17, 'he [the covenant Lord] will rejoice over you with gladness; he will quiet you by his love; he will exult over you with loud singing'. If God's word did not agree with Owen we would think he was immeasurably over-stating the truth. How could our

[1] Quoted in Sinclair B. Ferguson, *John Owen and the Christian Life* (Edinburgh: Banner of Truth, 1987), p. 18.

Saviour possibly be glad in us 'without sorrow'? Because we are his; loved by him in eternity, redeemed by his own blood, sanctified by his Spirit, his own 'brothers' (*Heb.* 2:11). Let that astonishing truth be the means of drawing out from you those 'returns of love' that the Beloved seeks from his Bride.

23. *Faith, the Protestant Watchword*

Some years ago I attended the Annual Cambridge Lecture sponsored by the Protestant Truth Society. Sadly, we live in a day when that once (and still) noble word 'Protestant' has fallen on hard times. (The word Protestant is derived from the Latin *protestari* meaning publicly declare. Historically, the word originated in the letter of protestation by Lutheran princes against the decision of the Diet of Speyer in 1529, which reaffirmed the edict at the Diet of Worms of 1521 banning Luther's writings). Part of the reason, no doubt, is that the word has been hijacked by politically-minded people, many of whom are strangers to true Protestantism.

However, there is a deeper, more lamentable reason why this venerable word has fallen on hard times — we live in a nation that is profoundly ignorant of its history. And the nation that forgets its history has lost its moorings and is heading for disaster.

Let me make one point before I go any further, just in case you think this is a plea for us to yearn for the past. I am no antiquarian. We live in the twenty-first century, not the sixteenth or seventeenth. God is the living God, he is not tied to any era of history, however blessed (though even the most blessed of past eras were punctuated with spiritual and moral ignorance and declension). However, to be ignorant of history, is to be ignorant of God. History is *His-story* (trite maybe, but profoundly true). There is a constant refrain in Deuteronomy that makes the point: again and again the Lord commands his church to 'remember', not to forget his past goodness, mercy, and kindness. A sense of history is essential for authentic, faithful Christian living.

The lecture I heard illustrated what I am saying. The title was 'John Rogers: Proto-Martyr of the English Reformation'. To my shame, I had never heard of John Rogers (being a Scotsman, I have some excuse—perhaps!). Rogers lived in a day when simply to teach your children the Ten Commandments in English put you in jeopardy of your life. Because he was an unyielding 'Protestant', a man who put the authority of the Bible above and before the authority of Queen Mary ('Bloody Mary') and Parliament, he was burned at the stake. He had a wife and eleven children, but not even for their poor sakes would he recant his evangelical faith. Indeed, it was his wife and children who pressed him to be faithful unto death! Whatever else he was, John Rogers was a man who took Jesus Christ seriously—and it cost him his life. In laying down his life, Rogers was simply following in the footsteps of an eminent company of men and women throughout the ages who 'were tortured, refusing to accept release, so that they might rise again to a better life . . . of whom the world was not worthy' (*Heb*.11:35ff.). This is our history. The cause of the gospel is not advanced by faint hearts.

But what has all this to do with us today, living as we do in the twenty-first century? Everything. The enemies of the gospel in the West today do not burn us at the stake, they just ridicule, marginalise, and demonise us. Absolute truth is mocked—except of course the absolute truth of humanistic relativism (*i.e.*, 'anything goes'!). Let us not be in any doubt that faithfulness to our Lord Jesus today will be costly (*John* 15:18ff.). No-one will burn you at the stake, perhaps, but there are other costs that are sore and wounding to bear.

We live in a post-Christian culture, much like the culture into which the Christian church was born. It was not faint-heartedness that caused the world to be turned upside down by the early Christians. They confronted their godless world with great grace and great boldness: 'We must obey God rather than men' was their unshakeable conviction (*Acts* 5:29). What was it God blessed in their labours?—their courageous proclamation of the gospel in the power of the Holy Spirit. This is what shook godless Corinth and delivered sin-blinded, morally-depraved men and women from their bondage to Satan, and brought them into the light and liberty of the kingdom of Jesus Christ—'and such *were* some of you, but you were washed . . .' (*1 Cor.* 6:9-11). When John Knox was asked to account for the remarkable events of the Scottish Reformation of 1560, he replied, 'God gave his Holy Spirit to simple men in great abundance.'

History teaches us that no matter how degenerate a people may be, the gospel is the power of God for salvation. God is the God of history. His 'footprints' are all over history—if we have the eyes of faith to see them. But those 'footprints' were often sprinkled with the blood of faithful Christians. So, let us then 'be steadfast, immovable, always abounding in the work of the Lord, knowing that in the Lord your labour is not in vain' (*1 Cor.* 15:58). Our Lord Jesus was obedient unto death, and he is 'the founder and perfecter of our faith' (*Heb.* 12:2).

24. *Faith's Present Experience*

'MAN is an enigma, whose only solution can be found in God.'[1] So wrote Herman Bavinck, the great Dutch theologian. What Bavinck wrote is

[1] Herman Bavinck, *Our Reasonable Faith*, (Grand Rapids: Baker, 1977), p. 23.

immediately applicable to fallen men and women. Science cannot explain who and what we are. Science cannot tell us what will ultimately become of us. It cannot explain the mystery that is man, for we are a mystery, even a contradiction. When science (so-called) seeks to explain us in purely humanistic, evolutionary terms, we rebel. We know that we are more than a chance amalgam of sub-atomic particles. We know, even when we do not want to acknowledge it, that there is more to us than meets the eye! Man is an enigma whose only solution is to be found in God.

What is less obvious to many Christians, however, is that what Bavinck writes is no less applicable to believers. There is, even in the most blessed of Christians, a perplexity that can at times be overwhelming. We get a glimpse of this perplexity in Paul's confession in Romans 7:15ff.: 'for I do not understand my own actions. For I do not do what I want, but I do the very thing I hate . . . Wretched man that I am!' Paul is an enigma to himself. He is deeply perplexed by the contradiction of his life.

Paul was not some abnormal, unspiritual, Spirit-deficient Christian. He was acknowledging the inescapable tension that lies within the heart and life of every true believer. He is a child of God, but yet marked by frail, fallen flesh. He is an heir of God's glory, but yet encompassed with weakness. He is united to Jesus Christ, the Lord of glory, but living in an environment ruled and defaced by the devil. He is a sanctified Christian, but is troubled, and at times all but overwhelmed, by indwelling sin. The Christian is an enigma whose only solution is to be found in God. This is Paul's conclusion in Romans 7:24, 25: 'Who will deliver me from this body of death? Thanks be to God through Jesus Christ our Lord!'

The enigma and contradiction will not last forever. Our union with the glorified God-Man is the guarantee that we will all, one coming day, share in his 'perfect resolution'. Now we 'groan inwardly as we wait eagerly for adoption as sons' (*Rom.* 8:23). The day has not yet arrived when our lowly bodies will be transformed to be like his glorious body (*Phil.* 3:21), but that day is coming, for God has ordained it, and the triumph of the Saviour assures it!

We live at the intersection of two worlds—this fallen world which is passing away, and the world to come which has already come in the Persons of our Lord Jesus Christ and the Holy Spirit, both of whom were sent from the Father. There is therefore an inescapable ache in every truly Christian heart: we are not yet home. And that ache is at times heightened by the aggravations of indwelling sin and the assaults of the devil. So much so, that we can think that because we do not do what we long to do, but do what we hate to do, we cannot possibly be Christians. If we are not grieved and humbled by this indwelling enigma, we should seriously ask ourselves whether indeed we can possibly be Christians. But if you are perplexed and humbled by your contradictions, and grieve over the inconsistencies and contradictions in your life, I would suggest you evidence one of the marks of authentic saving faith.

I write these lines not to excuse our contradictions, but to cheer, with hope, the heart of any saint who is burdened by their contradictions. One day the Lord will finally deliver all his people from their 'body of death'. Then we will cease to be wretched men and women (who are at the same time sons of the living God); instead we will be glorified saints, with all our enigmas and contradictions forever expunged from our lives, conformed perfectly to the likeness of our Saviour Jesus Christ.

25. Faith's Great Comfort

Contrary to what Open Theists (or Free-will Theists) would have us believe, the God of the Bible is perfectly omniscient. He knows all things, and knows all things because he ordained all things (*Eph.* 1:11). As the Psalmist reminds us, 'Our God is in the heavens; he does all that he pleases' (*Psa.* 115:3). This does not mean that Christians have easy, ready answers to every genuine searching question. God's absolute sovereignty deeply humbles us and, with Paul, leaves us out of our depth (see *Rom.* 11:33-36). There are, however, at least two truths that are embedded in God's sovereignty that bring the deepest comfort and hope to believers: history is under God's control and it follows God's plan.

Contrary to how things may often appear, 'our God reigns'. History is not a chain of random events. History is the fulfilling of God's will and purpose. We see this quite starkly put in the Book of Habakkuk. God's church, the southern kingdom of Judah, was being threatened by the Chaldeans (Babylonians). But look how the Lord himself impressed on his prophet that what was happening was under the sovereign Lord's control; 'I am raising up the Chaldeans, that ruthless and impetuous people, who sweep across the whole earth' (*Hab.* 1:6). This world super-power, was gaining power and hegemony, not because of its own prowess or strategic gifts, but because the sovereign Lord decreed it. This is a theme repeated regularly throughout the Scriptures: 'His dominion is an eternal dominion ... He does as he pleases with the powers of heaven and the peoples of the earth' (*Dan.* 4:35). Our God reigns. However tangled and confused history may appear, God is in control. Of course, here we live by faith and not by sight. But such faith in God's sovereign control is not illusory.

In the cross of our Lord Jesus Christ we see apparent unbridled wickedness brutalising the Lord of glory, but doing so only according to 'God's set purpose and foreknowledge' (*Acts* 2:23). And out of that apparent unbridled wickedness, God provided for a world of lost sinners a salvation for all who believe. History is never for one moment outside God's perfect, holy, sovereign, and gracious control.

History is under God's control, but no less does it follow God's plan. What is happening now in the world with Iraq, Afghanistan, and the Arab world, is no accident. It is all part of God's eternal plan. History has a purposeful trajectory. Every step fits in to the eternal plan. And what is that plan? Ultimately, it is to establish God's kingdom and God's King. Since the fall of Adam in the garden, God has been at work establishing his kingdom in the world. This was the vision given to Daniel:

> In the time of those kings, the God of heaven will
> set up a kingdom that will never be destroyed . . .
> It will crush all those kingdoms and bring them to
> an end, but it will itself endure forever (*Dan.* 2:44).

Every world event, every local happening, every personal circumstance has an eternal purpose to it. It doesn't matter that we cannot always see the purpose (in fact, we rarely do!). It is enough to know that our gracious God has his plan — and by his grace we are at the heart of it in Christ.

God's absolute sovereignty in history, cosmic and personal, is the greatest comfort to Christian believers. Not because we have, as it were, the 'inside-track' on world events; but rather because it means that our loving Father, gracious Saviour, and indwelling Holy Spirit, are in control. One day the purpose and the plan will shine in all its unspotted glory and wisdom. Then we shall know, even as also we are known. Until then, be of good cheer fellow Christian: your God reigns!

26. *What Faith Aspires To*

The church of Christ is full of unsung heroes. They do not, on the whole, possess the kind of spiritual gifts that get them noticed and give them 'a name'. They are, at least in my experience, rarely the most intellectually able or theologically articulate Christians in a congregation. And yet, they give their congregations a spiritual lustre that is nothing less than a divine benediction. Perhaps you are already wondering just who these people are; let me tell you, they are the spiritual seed of 'Barnabas', the proto-typical 'Son of Encouragement' (see *Acts* 4:36).

The grace of encouragement is a precious and much to be prized grace. It is a grace that owes its origin, as all graces do, to the indwelling presence of the Divine Encourager, the Holy Spirit. Indeed, the Holy Spirit is called the 'Paraclete', the One who comes alongside to minister the grace of Christ to his needy, wounded, limping servants. To be an encourager, is to be the Holy Spirit's chosen instrument to minister God's grace to his often beleaguered saints. This is surely a grace that all Christians should aspire to. It may not, and probably will not, get you 'a name'; it will, however, make you a precious instrument for good to your fellow believers.

Why are 'sons [and daughters] of encouragement' so rare in our churches (granted that your church may be an exception)? A number of reasons spring to mind.

The first is, too many of us are taken up with ourselves, our needs, our concerns, our problems, our struggles. Encouragers, by definition, think more about the needs of others than their own needs. Encouragers are not free of personal struggles and trials; but they put the needs of others before their own needs. They heed the apostolic command to 'look not only to your own interests, but also to the interests of others'. In doing this, they display the selflessness of the Saviour.

A second reason is that too many of us are primed to search out weaknesses and flaws in other Christians, than primed to minister the consolation of Christ. Encouragers have Christ-like sight and a Christ-like heart. They are not blind to the sins and weaknesses in fellow Christians, but they recognize that 'love builds up'. This, no doubt, can become an excuse to neglect the grace of rebuke. But the rebukes that make their God-ordained mark on our lives, are those rebukes administered by the church's encouragers—it is the wounds of friends that are most taken to heart. Too often in the church, those who are most eagle-eyed at pointing out what is wrong, are usually the very people who should never do the pointing out. Our Lord Jesus memorably impressed this on us with his teaching on 'specks' and 'planks' (see *Matt.* 7:3-5).

In the third place, encouragers appear to be few in the church because we do not take as seriously as we should the present High-Priestly ministry of our Saviour. As he exercises his heavenly ministry from the throne of grace, our Lord Jesus 'sympathizes with our weaknesses'. He never forgets that we are dust. He knows perfectly our flaws and failures, but he deals with us compassionately and mercifully. There is a tender humanity about our majestic Saviour. Encouragers are often our great High Priest's means of ministering his divine sympathy to our bruised and lacerated souls.

You do not need a degree in theology to be an encourager. You do, however, need a Christ-like spirit. You do not need to be a gifted speaker or an extrovert personality to be an encourager. You do, however, need a humble spirit, that doesn't wait for others to do good to you before you do good to them. Indeed, the grace of encouragement only grows in the fertile soil of humility. A kind and thoughtful word, a few lines on a note (not an e-mail!), an assurance of prayer, an unexpected visit, a smile, a thoughtful enquiry after some major event. None of these require you to have read Calvin,

Owen, Edwards, or Lloyd-Jones. They do require you to have drunk deeply of the grace of the Lord Jesus Christ. May it please the Lord to adorn our churches with encouragers. Our fellowships will be the sweeter and more wholesome.

27. Faith's Present Ache

The longing for happiness is etched indelibly in every human heart. We seek for happiness, we ache for happiness and we will do almost anything to secure happiness. Our problem is, however, that most people neither know what happiness is, nor where they can find it. Sin has blinded our minds, corrupted our hearts and left us 'eyeless seekers'. Herman Bavinck, the great Dutch theologian, put it memorably:

> All men are really seeking after God . . . but they do not all seek Him in the right way, nor at the right place. They seek Him down below, and He is up above. They seek Him on the earth, and He is in heaven. They seek Him afar, and He is nearby. They seek Him in money, in property, in fame, in power, and in passion; and He is to be found in the high and holy places, and with him that is of a contrite and humble spirit (*Isa.* 57:15) . . . They

seek Him and at the same time they flee Him . . . In this, as Pascal so profoundly pointed out, consists the greatness and miserableness of man. He longs for truth and is false by nature. He yearns for rest and throws himself from one diversion upon another. He pants for a permanent and eternal bliss and seizes on the pleasures of the moment. He seeks for God and loses himself in the creature.[1]

What a picture of the world we live in — always searching, but never finding. Why is this? In all of the searching after happiness there is a fundamental assumption. The assumption is that 'science' can explain and fulfil this longing. The evolutionary hypothesis, so vigorously promoted by professed atheists like Richard Dawkins, maintains that we are all chance amalgams of sub-atomic particles, mere carbon units that have no meaning, and no ultimate significance. The longing after happiness is thus reduced to a mere biological impulse, which can be satisfied by other biological impulses. The horizon of happiness is 'under the sun', and the pursuit of happiness 'under the sun' becomes the uncritically accepted goal of most men and women.

There is, however, a fundamental flaw in this analysis: science cannot explain the nature of and the contradiction in men and women. We know we are more than mere carbon units. The Bible tells us what that 'more' is. We all know there is more to us than meets the eye.

[1] Bavinck, *Our Reasonable Faith*, p. 22.

Satan seeks tirelessly to blind the minds of unbelievers (2 *Cor.* 4:4) and our guilty, rebel-consciences 'suppress the truth' we know to be true (*Rom.* 1:18). The truth that science cannot reckon with and can know nothing of is the truth of our divine origin and our profound fall. The deepest truth about us all is that God has set eternity in our hearts; he has made us in his own image, and even in our fallenness the faint echoes of these truths resonate in the dark recesses of our souls. To quote Bavinck again, 'Man is an enigma whose solution can be found only in God.'[1]

The happiness we all long for is not found in anything 'under the sun'; it is found in fellowship with him who made the sun! The first Psalm puts it simply and yet profoundly:

> Blessed [truly happy] is the man who does not walk in the counsel of the wicked or stand in the way of sinners or sit in the seat of mockers. But his delight is in the law of the LORD and on his law he meditates day and night. He is like a tree planted by streams of water, which yields its fruit in season and whose leaf does not wither. Whatever he does prospers' (NIV).

Happiness, soul-fulfilling, heart-engaging happiness, is found in the friendship of the 'blessed [or happy] God' (*1 Tim.* 6:15) and in feeding upon his word. This

---

[1] Bavinck, *Our Reasonable Faith*, p. 23.

explains the mission of God's Son: 'I came that they may have life and have it abundantly' (*John* 10:10).

The happiness we all ache for is an eternal happiness. It could hardly be otherwise when God has put eternity in our hearts (*Eccles.* 3:11). So, fellow Christian, 'Seek the things that are above, where Christ is' (*Col.* 1:1). Nothing and no-one under the sun can give you what your heart longs for. Happiness is having the happy God filling your heart with his glorious presence.

28. *The Tenderness of Faith*

When our Lord Jesus came to the tomb where Lazarus lay dead, he wept (*John* 11:35). Our Lord knew better than anyone that God is sovereign. He knew that Lazarus' death was not an unfortunate happenstance but part of God's sovereign plan. He knew that everything God does is good and right. But when he came to Lazarus' place of burial, 'Jesus wept'. The Holy Spirit could not have inspired a more blessedly reassuring text for Christians to reflect on and take immense hope and encouragement from. Two things in particular call for comment.

First, the life of faith is not coldly stoical. If our Lord Jesus, the man of faith *par excellence*, wept over the death of a friend (and over the impending divine judgment that was soon to fall upon unbelieving sinners, *Luke* 19:41), then we see that the life of faith at its best and highest is marked by tenderness and deeply-felt heart-sympathy. Having a high conviction concerning God's absolute sovereignty does not in any sense make the Christian believer an unmoved observer of the human condition. Faith and tears are not mutually exclusive; indeed, they are blood relations. Faith brings us into union with the One who wept. Of all people, Christians should be the most tender-hearted. The last thing anyone should be able to accuse us of is coldness or disinterestedness. We are to 'weep with those who weep' (*Rom.* 12:15). We are to 'be imitators of God as beloved children' (*Eph.* 5:1), and our God is a God who is afflicted in all our afflictions (*Isa.* 63:9). God is not a detached heavenly stoic. He is not the great Unmoved Mover of the Deists. He is a God of demonstrative love who 'did not spare his own Son but gave him up for us all' (*Rom.* 5:8; 8:32).

Too often some Christians have felt that tears and distress were marks of unbelief. The truth is they marked the life of the proto-typical man of faith, our sinless, glorious Saviour, Jesus Christ. The true life of faith is marked by tenderness of heart. It can hardly be otherwise if we are united to the man of faith, Jesus Christ. If we can remain coldly distant and unmoved in the face of human need, there is something deeply and profoundly amiss with us. 'Jesus wept', and we can and must weep too.

Secondly, the life of faith can count on the tender compassion of Christ in all its times of need. Christians are not excused the sufferings of this present time (*Rom.* 8:18). We know the pain of unexpected loss, of shattered hopes, of broken promises, of bitter failure. We feel the pain of helplessness as our children go through trials and struggles that all but overwhelm them. Is it not the greatest comfort to know in the midst of our pains, yes that God is sovereign, but that his sovereignty is merciful and tender towards his people? 'In all their affliction he was afflicted.'

Since the incarnation, we have a Saviour who knows our frame not merely by perfect omniscience, but also by personal experience. Our great High Priest is able to sympathise with our weaknesses because he has been tempted in every way, just as we are, yet was without sin (*Heb.* 4:15, 16). There is dust on the throne of heaven; glorified dust but yet dust. And 'he knows our frame, he remembers that we are dust' (*Psa.* 103:14).

This side of glory we are left to wrestle, at times, with quite bewildering providences. God's ways are not our ways. Sometimes his ways leave us perplexed, pained. Some well meaning saint might say, 'Snap out of it; don't you know God is sovereign?' Thankfully, 'Jesus wept', and wept with those who wept. What makes God's unfathomable sovereignty bearable and even comfortable for the believer, is the knowledge that it is the sovereignty of One who weeps, who is afflicted in all our afflictions. Sometimes all we have are tears, but tears belong to the essence of the life of faith. They marked the perfect faith of our Lord Jesus Christ.

29. Faith's Submissiveness

During Samuel Rutherford's time in London, where he was a delegate from the Church of Scotland at the Westminster Assembly, two children from his second marriage died. He wrote sorrowfully of this to another bereaved parent:

> I was in your condition; I had but two children, and both are dead since I came hither . . . The good husbandman may pluck His roses, and gather in His lilies at mid-summer, and, for aught I dare say, in the beginning of the first summer month . . . [1]

What is so striking about Rutherford's letter is its humble submissiveness to God's sore providence. To lose one child would be the sorest of trials; to lose two in quick succession must have been an unimaginable trial. Some will no doubt be thinking, 'In those days death was a more everyday fact of life than it is today; it was not uncommon for children to die in infancy.' True. But do you think that a Christian father or mother

[1] Rutherford, *Letters*, p. 621.

could ever easily and painlessly lose even one of their children? However common or inevitable the death of a loved one is, their death pierces our heart. Love does not easily give up to death the one it loves. But Rutherford's letter speaks to us of a man who, though his heart is aching, humbly submits to the wise, gracious, and loving sovereignty of 'the Good Husbandman' (*John* 15:1).

It is one of the most evident, and sweetest, marks of saving faith, that the Lord enables us to acquiesce humbly and not grudgingly in the face of dark and sore providences. To be able to say, 'the Lord gave and the Lord has taken away, blessed be the name of the Lord', is a mark of faith at its purest and highest (*Job* 1:21). None of this is a mere matter of temperament. On the contrary, such humble, submissive faith is the fruit of a heart that has begun to grasp the grace of the Lord Jesus Christ.

The whole course of our Saviour's life was a course of humble submissive obedience to his Father's will. Never once did our Lord Jesus murmur or complain as he endured reviling, rejection, slander, and worse. Rather, he entrusted 'himself to him who judges justly' (*1 Pet.* 2:23). Our Saviour is the experiential model of humble submissive faith and it is God's predestinating purpose to conform us to his Son's likeness. That 'likeness' is nowhere more beautifully and movingly etched for us than in Philippians 2:5ff. There we see the selfless humility of Jesus, who 'made himself nothing' and humbled himself, becoming 'obedient to the point of death, even death on a cross'. As in faith he walked the pathway of unimaginable suffering, our Saviour never once complained, never once questioned the love of his Father. Even in the Garden of Gethsemane, as the dawning reality of the cross began to pierce his soul, he prays, 'Not my will, but your will be done' (*Luke* 22:42). The essence of faith is trust; and to the end Jesus trusted his Father.

It is union with the humbly submissive Jesus Christ that believers are brought into through the gospel. Those believers whose faith most glorifies God, are not those who fluently can talk about it, or insightfully write about it, or passionately preach about it, but those who humbly trust God when all around their soul is giving way. God's ways are not our ways. He is God. His purposes towards his people are the product of his perfect wisdom, gracious sovereignty and electing love. Here we see through a glass darkly. Here, our fragile, earthen vessels are only too easily cracked by perplexity and pain. What will keep us from losing heart, and complaining bitterly, is the persuasion that the One 'who did not spare his own Son but gave him up for us all . . . will also with him graciously give us all things' (*Rom.* 8:32).

The quiet dignity of a 'bruised reed', humbled under God's almighty hand, is a beautiful sight to behold. It is a testimony to the grace and love of an unseen God. It tells the people of God that God can be trusted, even when all earthly hopes are dashed. Such grace truly is a 'rare jewel'; it sparkles and gives lustre to every Christian profession.

30. Dealing With Our Past: Trusting God

Many Christians are haunted by their past. It can tyrannise them, paralyse them, and all but crush the life out of them. It is undeniably true that one of Satan's many anti-Christian devices is his bringing our past to remembrance, to humble us, distract us, turn us in upon ourselves, and leave us with a paralysing sense of guilt and shame. How are we to react and respond when Satan placards our past before us?

The very first thing we must do is to apply afresh to our disturbed minds and shamed spirits the glorious truth that God in Christ remembers our sins no more. However scarlet our sinful past, the atoning blood of Christ has washed us whiter than snow. How very basic this is, and yet how precious! I have often thought of those soul-stirring words of Paul in 1 Corinthians 6:11, 'And such were some of you. But you were washed, you were sanctified, you were justified in the name of the Lord Jesus Christ and by the Spirit of our God.' We live in a world soiled by the grossness, wickedness, and filth of sin. Multitudes have been deceived by the 'deceitfulness of sin'. How much it offers, how alluring it appears, but how deadly it actually is! What are we to say to men and women whose lives have been shamed and soiled by idolatry, immorality, adultery, homosexuality, greed, drunkenness, and addictions of all kinds? Surely this: 'the blood of Jesus [God's] Son cleanses us from *all* sin' (*1 John* 1:7). This was Paul's message to those believers in Corinth: This is where we must always begin. However gory your past, however shameful, filthy, and vile, God has provided in his own Son and by his atoning sacrifice, the cleansing sinners need.

We should secondly remember this, 'Who shall bring any charge against God's elect? It is God who justifies' (*Rom.* 8:33). Think of all who can bring charges against you: Satan, this world, your own conscience. And then think on this: God has justified you in Christ, you who trust in Jesus! In God's eyes, and this is so staggering that we almost hesitate to say it, you are as just, as righteous as Christ himself! Pause for a moment and take this in: God 'made him to be sin who knew no sin, so that in him we might become the righteousness of God' (*2 Cor.* 5:21). Do you wonder why this message is called *gospel?* By nature and practice we are guilty, vile, damnable, rebel sinners. Maybe you are thinking, 'O, but Ian if you only knew my past and the sins . . .' My friend, even you do not know how vile you were! You think your sins were black and shameful? They were infinitely more black and shameful than you will ever know. But, 'God is rich in mercy'. He does not treat us as our sins deserve. Hallelujah!

The believer's past has been wiped clean and covered by the infinite avalanche of the Saviour's obedience and blood. Our past has been redeemed. Christ nailed it to his cross when he bore all our sin and shame and God's holy curse upon them. Satan will always want you to 'look in' to yourself; God wants you always to 'look out and up' to Christ. Perhaps you are asking, 'Always? What about "Examine yourselves to see whether you are in the faith"?' (2 *Cor.* 13:5). Yes, Christians are on occasion to 'look in', but never without ceasing in doing so to 'look out and up'. It is from the wonder of our glorious union with Christ that we 'look in'. But are we not to 'remember and not forget' our past? (see *Deut.* 9:6ff). Yes—but only to remind us of our deep unworthiness and the even deeper grace of God that has saved us and kept us.

These have been basic, very basic thoughts. And yet, is it not true that when we stumble it is usually because we have forgotten what is most basically true of us?

> When Satan tempts me to despair
>   And tells me of the guilt within;
> Upward I look and see him there,
>   Who made an end of all my sin.[1]

Be encouraged my brothers and sisters in Christ.

---

[1] From Charitie Lees De Chenez's hymn, 'Before the throne of God above'.

31. Faith in a Post-modern World

Peter Marshall was a Scotsman who became Chaplain to the United States Senate. He wrote some words that speak powerfully to our morally-decaying society and to an evangelical Christianity that has its focus on all the wrong things:

> The modern challenge to motherhood is the eternal challenge—that of being a godly woman. The very phrase sounds strange in our ears. We never hear it now. We hear about every other type of women: beautiful women, smart women, sophisticated women, career women, talented women, divorced women. But so seldom do we hear of a godly woman—or of a godly man either, for that matter. I believe women come nearer to fulfilling their God-given function in the home than anywhere else. It is a much nobler thing to be a good wife, than to be Miss America. It is a greater achievement to establish a Christian home than it is to produce a second-rate novel filled with filth. It is a far, far better thing in the realms of morals to be old fashioned, than to be ultra-modern. The world has enough women who know how to be smart. It needs women who are willing to be simple. The world has enough women who know how to be brilliant. It needs some who will be brave. The world has enough women who are popular. It needs more who are pure. We need

women, and men too, who would rather be morally right than socially correct.

I wonder how you react to these words? You could tell a lot about the state of your spiritual life, I think, by your reaction to Marshall's analysis.

Christian virtue is rarely eclipsed overnight. Usually it is eviscerated by the slow process of becoming conformed to the prevailing pattern of the age. If you live in the midst of squalor, and everyone around you sees the squalor as normal, it takes unyielding courage and conviction to stand against the squalor and resist its embrace. Too often today evangelicalism dresses itself in the world's clothes in the hope that it may thereby gain a hearing for the gospel. Now, it is true that Christians are to become 'all things to all people, that by all means [we] might save some' (*1 Cor.* 9:22). But in no sense does this mean that we are to share the world's values and lifestyle. Consider our Lord Jesus Christ. He exemplified what it meant to identify with this fallen, sinful world: 'And the Word became flesh' (*John* 1:14). He shared the frailty and vulnerability of our humanity. He entered into the darkness of our sinful predicament. And yet he remained 'holy, innocent, unstained, separated from sinners' (*Heb.* 7:26). He shared our condition, but not our sin. Indeed, he never once temporised, or tried to hide the absolute moral standards of God from sinners. What he said was given authority by who and what he was.

We live in an age that is seeking wilfully to subvert the biblical foundations of society. At the heart of those foundations are the God-ordained roles of godly male headship, and godly female submission. It is tragically true that many men, Christian men, have abdicated their God-ordained calling in their homes and made it difficult for their wives lovingly to submit to their headship. Nothing would more persuade a Christian woman to rise to her God-ordained calling than having a husband who loves her as Christ loves his church, who loves her children, and who, faithfully, gently, and unyieldingly leads the family in making God's word and not the world's enticements, the pattern of life.

It may well be costly—indeed it certainly will be costly—but Christians must 'dare to be different'. First, of course, for God's honour and glory. Second, for the good of our own souls: 'Do not be conformed to this world, but be transformed by the renewal of your mind' (*Rom.* 12:2). But thirdly, if we do not dare to be different (*i.e.*, live the values of God's word), then our evangelical testimony will be little more than hollow, pathetic words that the world will mock and ignore.

I have recently finished reading Brian Moynihan's biography of William Tyndale. My abiding impression of this fine work is that Tyndale, and others like him (*e.g.*, the English Reformer John Frith) dared to be different. They refused to fit in with the prevailing ethos and expectations of their society. It cost them their lives, but the impact of their lives for the sake of Christ and the gospel was enormous.

Dare to be different! Not to draw attention to yourself. Not to show your Christian brothers how 'Reformed' you are. Dare to be different because the gospel of your Saviour has brought you into the ethic of a better world, whose King is the Lord God Almighty. Live to please him.

32. The Humbling Fact that Pervades the Life of Faith

The Bible is a remarkable book. Supremely, of course, because it is the revelation of the one true God and makes us wise for salvation through faith in our Lord Jesus Christ (2 *Tim.* 3:15). There is, however, another remarkable feature about the Bible that I would like to reflect on with you.

When the Holy Spirit set about the work of infallibly inspiring men to pen God's saving revelation, he ensured that what they wrote was the truth, the whole truth, and nothing but the truth. That meant that God's 'pen-men' did not leave out the follies and sins of God's people. Nowhere does the Scripture attempt to airbrush the failures and disobedience of believers out of the picture. Indeed, it almost seems at times that their sins and failures are unnecessarily placarded before our eyes. Who of us would have included the Book of Judges in God's word, especially its latter chapters? Who of us would not have wanted to hide from view the sins of men like Samson, a man the Bible calls a hero of faith? The Holy Spirit, thankfully, was not so squeamish. In often technicolour intensity, he plots the sinful follies of even the choicest of God's saints. Why is this?

There are a number of reasons, but one stands out: through the manifest weaknesses and sins of believers, God impresses on us the true character of the life of faith. Believing in the Lord Jesus Christ does not lift you out of the struggles, trials, and temptations that are native to life this side of glory. Faith at its best and purest is punctuated with folly and sin. The most favoured and privileged of Christians fall and fail. This may seem to some an excuse to go on sinning. However, to quote Paul, anyone who thinks like this, 'Their condemnation is just' (*Rom.* 3:8). Perfection awaits us in heaven's glory. This fact not only breathes realism into the believer, it armours their heart against the heady varieties of perfectionism that are always (sadly) afflicting Christ's church.

The life of faith is lived out in sinful bodies. It has not pleased the Lord to eradicate sin from our lives while we yet live in this world. There are remnants of corruption in us that are a landing ground for Satan's deceitful temptations. We all know the truth of the hymn,

Prone to wander, Lord, I feel it,
  Prone to leave the God I love.[1]

The trouble often is, however, that when we sin and fail, we too easily listen to the lies of the enemy of our souls and perhaps begin to question whether it is possible for such a privileged Christian to sin and fail as we have done. But it is—look at Abraham, Jacob, Samson, Peter (the list is almost endless). God has mercifully allowed his choicest people's sins to be written in 'large letters' for our encouragement! Yes, for our humbling, 'let anyone who thinks that he stands take heed lest he fall' (*1 Cor.* 10:12); but also for our encouraging. God did not give up on his people, he continued in grace to persevere with them.

The life of faith is not even, untroubled, effortless. On the contrary, it is punctuated with many a fall. But the last word never lies with our falls, but with the One who is 'rich in mercy'.

I am conscious that what I have written could be used as an excuse to live at a 'low level', never aspiring to grow up into Christ who is the Head, tolerating sins that need to be put to death by the Spirit's power (*Rom.* 8:13)—May it never be! Rather, may we see God's great kindness in allowing us to glimpse the struggles and falls of his most eminent saints and the astonishing grace that picked them up, forgave them freely, and set them on their way again.

[1] From Robert Robinson's hymn, 'Come, Thou fount of every blessing'.

33. Faith and Numbers

Have you ever wondered why Luke tells us in Acts about 'numbers'? At Pentecost 'there were added that day about three thousand souls' (*Acts* 2:41), and 'the Lord added to their number day by day' (2:47). In Acts 4 we are told that 'the number of men came to about five thousand' (verse 4) and in chapter 5, we read, 'and more than ever believers were added to the Lord, multitudes of both men and women' (verse 14). So Luke continues throughout Acts, telling us that, everywhere the gospel went, numbers (large as well as small) were added to the church.

In the Reformed church we are not comfortable with 'numbers'. We say that it is not numbers that matter but faithfulness: and we are right to say so. The danger, however, is that by this route we come to develop an 'unexpectant mindset'. We see our smallness and assume that 'small is beautiful'; the more truly Reformed we are, the smaller we inevitably will be. But this contentment with a faithful (and small) remnant may hide a deep spiritual malaise within our hearts.

It may hide the fact that we are a prayerless church (or pastor). James tells us, 'You do not have, because you do not ask God.' The reason why many of our churches, at least in the UK, are so small, may be because we 'do not ask God' to add to our numbers. Do we really believe that God hears and answers prayer?

That he is able 'to do immeasurably more than all we ask or imagine'? Are we wrestling with God for his saving blessings to be showered upon us? Isaiah lamented the spiritual barrenness in his own day and cried, 'No-one calls on your name or strives to lay hold of you.' My brothers and sisters in Christ, do we *really* pray?

Or, it may be that when we pray, God does not give us what we ask 'because [we] ask with wrong motives' (*James* 4:3). One motive alone inclines God's ear to our prayers—his own glory and particularly the glory of his Son. Everything our Saviour did, he did to bring glory to his Father. Is this the burning motivation that shines like a beacon in our churches? Why do we want to see sinners saved and added to the church? To give our church a profile it presently lacks? To vindicate our Reformed convictions? Is the truth not that in our churches we have little felt passion for the glory of our God? Does it deeply pain us, humble us, and shame us, that people we meet every day live as if there were no God, that Jesus Christ is a name to blaspheme, not a name to love and adore? The great evangelists we all so admire, were marked by a restless longing for the glory of Jesus Christ. They besought heaven, and God blessed their labours abundantly. Yes, they were favoured men; but why were they so favoured? If nothing else, ponder that and be deeply challenged and humbled by their passion for God's glory.

One more thing comes to mind. Is it possible that our smallness is in any measure related to 'other things' eclipsing Jesus Christ as the absorbing focus of church life. How truly central is the love of God in Christ in our churches? My brother preachers, is the preaching of the cross of our Lord Jesus — its glory, grace, and love — the supreme note in our pulpit ministry? Is our chief boast, 'the cross of our Lord Jesus Christ'? My fellow Christian brothers and sisters, do we know in our own souls something of what Paul meant when he wrote, 'Christ's love compels us'? It was Christ's amazing love that made Paul the man he was; Christ's astonishing love defined everything about him. He was the evangelist he was because God's love had been poured into his heart by the Holy Spirit, and he could not rest until the world heard of this love. Too often in Reformed churches we end up majoring on minors and lose the plot. There are truths of 'first importance' and they all centre on the Person and mission of our Lord Jesus.

Please do not think for one moment that I am decrying smallness. I hope, rather, that I am asking myself first, and all who read this, *Are we small because we are content with smallness?* Numbers in themselves are meaningless. Many wonderful men and churches have laboured prayerfully, faithfully, and lovingly and seen little fruit for their labours. But is it not also true that if we expect little, we will receive little? Simply to wait and hope for revival to come can lead to present spiritual inertia.

Since the cross, resurrection, and ascension of our Lord Jesus we are no longer living in a day of small things! We are living in the days of a risen, regnant Saviour, to whom the Father has given all authority in heaven and on earth. Therefore, 'Ask and it shall be given to you.' May our gracious God stir us up today to give ourselves to prayer and a passion for his glory.

34. The Lips of the Faithful

One of the principal marks of a Christian is a bridled tongue that is under control. What we speak and how we speak reveals the measure of sanctification wrought in our hearts. 'Out of the overflow of the heart the mouth speaks' (*Matt.* 12:34).

It is quite remarkable to notice how often the New Testament highlights the significance of the tongue. Nowhere is this more prominent than in the Letter of James. The apostle says, 'How great a forest is set ablaze by such a small fire!'; and that the 'tongue is a fire, a world of unrighteousness. The tongue is set among our members, staining the whole body, setting on fire the entire course of life, and set on fire by hell . . . It is a restless evil, full of deadly poison' (3:5, 6, 8). These are shocking and sobering words. It hardly needs me to tell you how many relational animosities and congregational catastrophes have been caused by thoughtless, heartless, self-willed, ill-judged words.

What James is particularly concerned to impress on us is the utter incongruity of praising God and cursing men, who have been made in God's likeness, with the same tongue. 'My brothers, these things ought not to be so' (verse 10). Indeed, James goes further: 'Does a spring pour forth from the same opening both fresh and salt water?' (verse 11). The answer is an emphatic 'No'! To gossip about a fellow Christian, to malign his or her character, to seek to belittle them in public, to bring attention to their sins ('love covers a multitude of sins'!), is to behave like a pagan, not a Christian.

It is deeply challenging to read in Proverbs (where else?) that one of the distinguishing marks of the righteous is the conscientious way they use their tongues: 'The mouth of the righteous is a fountain of life (10:11) . . . The lips of the righteous feed many (10:21) . . . The lips of the righteous know what is acceptable (or fitting)' (10:32).

This last characteristic of the righteous tongue is especially important for believers to take to heart. It tells us that our speech as children of God should be 'measured'. It is only too easy to stray into verbal excess, to go over the top, to exaggerate. Christian speech is measured speech. It is thoughtful, not hasty. Once the word is out, it is like toothpaste out of the tube, impossible to recall.

But there is something more: Christian speech is 'appropriate' speech. Many things are best not said. Circumstances, people's personal or family situations, may well shout out to us (if we had ears to hear!) to hold our tongue. Some people embarrass easily and we need always to be asking ourselves, 'Is this necessary? Will it be kind? Will it be helpful?' Silence is golden, sometimes (see *Eccles.* 3:7). However, when we must speak, it is absolutely imperative that we learn the grace of appropriate speech.

'Appropriate speech' is, at heart, speech that seeks to build up, not tear down. It is in the context of a warning against the potential destructive capacities of the tongue that James draws attention to 'the wisdom that comes from above' (*James* 3:17). That wisdom, in contrast with the wisdom of the flesh, is 'first pure, then peaceable, gentle, open to reason, full of mercy and good fruits, impartial and sincere' (verse 17). These are the spiritual graces that are to style and shape the content that flows from our lips. This is not an *apologia* for insipid or anodyne speech. Christians are called to reprove and rebuke one another. But it is an imbedded fact of nature, as well as a gospel grace, that reproofs and rebukes are best received when they have been preceded by warm, generous encouragements: 'Faithful are the wounds of a *friend*' (*Prov.* 27:6)!

'The lips of the righteous know what is fitting.' On the contrary, 'a babbling fool will come to ruin' (*Prov.* 10:10). Quantity is never a substitute for quality. Measured, thoughtful, appropriate speech is a sweet grace.

Perhaps a few who read this might be thinking: 'Paul's words in Galatians 1:6-10 were not very measured!'

True—but it was appropriate in the context! There were men in the church who were denying the sole-saving sufficiency of the Lord Jesus Christ, who were denying that we are justified by grace alone, in and through Christ alone. To all such the church has always said, 'Anathema'. That is what the Bible calls 'fitting' speech.

35. Controversy and Faith

The Christian faith and controversy go hand in hand. Wherever the gospel of God's grace in Christ is planted it will inevitably provoke controversy and opposition. The reason is not hard to seek: the gospel confronts and provokes the sin-ingrained self-will and 'auto-soterism'[1] of this fallen, God-denying world. The armour-piercing truth of God's word is resisted and refused by men and women who 'love darkness instead of light because their deeds are evil'.

We see this controversy repeatedly in Jesus' encounters with sinners and Pharisees in the Gospel narratives. Jesus, God incarnate and full of grace, came to 'seek and save the lost'. He had not come to call the righteous but sinners to repentance. Like a doctor, his divine remit was

[1] The erroneous thinking that one has the ability to save one's self.

to help the sick, whoever they were. When Jesus called Levi to follow him, Levi hosted a 'conversion party' to celebrate God's great grace to him (*Mark* 2:13-17). To that party, Levi invited 'many tax collectors' and 'sinners' and Jesus, God's holy, impeccable Son, ate with this group of social and religious outcasts, which infuriated and scandalised the Pharisees. They could not understand why Jesus would ever come into contact with 'tax collectors' (rapacious Gentile collaborators) and 'sinners' (public disreputables). As a result, they were dismayed and disgusted. The root of the Pharisees' controversy with Jesus, however, went much deeper. They could not understand Jesus because they had a twisted and profoundly mistaken understanding of God.

To the Pharisees (the vast majority it would appear) God was a conditional God, whose favour was earned by religious performances. They looked on God's law as a ladder by which you could climb your way up and into his favour. They had little sense either of the holiness of God or the deep, ingrained sinfulness of man; they were practising semi-Pelagians.[1] The tragedy of this, of course, was that it was the utter contradiction of biblical

---

[1] Pelagianism was a heresy in the early church that Augustine confronted with vigour and passion. It was named after a British monk, Pelagius, who taught that men and women were not affected by Adam's sin and had the innate capacity to merit salvation from God. Semi-Pelagianism taught that salvation was achieved through faith in Christ *and* the merit of our good deeds. Roman Catholicism is Semi-Pelagian.

religion. Somehow, with the passing of the years, Judaism had separated God's grace from his commands. Law had been dislocated from its natural soil, the grace and love of God. Ethics had been divorced from theology. This, in part, led the Pharisees (literally, 'the separated ones') to isolate themselves from much of Jewish society, so as not to be religiously contaminated by people less ceremonially pure than they. How wrong they were. How blind they were to the whole covenant-breaking, formalising tendency of their nation's history. Throughout its history, God's church had often retreated into ritual, thinking that the cure for disobedience was 'a little more religion' (read *1 Sam.* 15:22, 23!).

How far removed from the gracious God of the Bible these Pharisees were. God's concern for his glory and purity among men had led him down through history to visit his sin-diseased people to heal them. Climactically, in the incarnation of his one and only Son, God 'made his dwelling among us'. He came into the midst of our sin-darkened world to reveal the glory of his 'grace and truth'. As the quaint Christmas hymn puts it, 'Love came down at Christmas' — gracious, sovereign-willed love. Jesus was an enigma to the Pharisees because they were strangers to the saving grace of God, the heritage and glory of their fathers, Abraham, Isaac and Jacob.

The example of our Lord Jesus is nothing less than a test of true religion: if we are not engaged 'among' the disreputables of this world, seeking, like our Saviour to call sinners to repentance, dare we call ourselves a

'Christian' church? Jesus was lambasted ('A glutton and a drunkard, a friend of tax collectors and sinners!', *Matt.* 11:19), misunderstood, plotted against; but he never wavered in seeking that which was lost. His great priority was saving sinners and went wherever he could find them. I have little doubt that the reason why my own heart is so little engaged with the disreputables of Cambridge is because I know little of the Saviour's love for lost perishing men and women. Compare the hours and energy we expend in getting our doctrine right and the hours and energy we spend in 'seeking' the lost. To quote our blessed Lord, 'We should have practised the latter, without neglecting the former' (*Matt.* 23:23, 24).

Jesus said, 'Follow me.' Whatever else that will mean, it surely means that we are called, in his name, to seek the lost. At the end of the day, to use the cliché, it really is ALL ABOUT GRACE!

36. *The Legacy that Faith Bequeaths*

A few years ago a young friend of mine died. Before he died he penned a 'Parting Letter' to his wife (175 pages!). The letter is a moving testimony of God's grace to a dying believer. As my friend concluded his letter he quoted these words of John Owen:

Jesus Christ is all, and in all; and where he is want-ing [lacking] there can be no good. Hunger cannot truly be satisfied without manna, the bread of life, which is Jesus Christ;—and what shall a hungry man do that hath no bread? Thirst cannot be quenched without that water or living spring, which is Jesus Christ;—and what shall a thirsty soul do without water? A captive, as we are all, cannot be delivered without redemption, which is Jesus Christ;—and what shall the prisoner do without his ransom? Fools, as we are all, cannot be instructed without wisdom, which is Jesus Christ;—without him we perish in our folly. All building without him is on the sand, which will surely fall. All working with-out him is in the fire, where it will be consumed. All riches without him have wings, and will away . . . A dungeon with Christ is a throne; and a throne without Christ, a hell. Nothing so ill, but Christ will compensate.[1]

Owen's words are worthy of careful meditation. He is impressing on us that none but Christ can satisfy. He is reminding us that our Lord Jesus 'is all in all'. He is encouraging us to make our Saviour our all in all. Surely we can never be reminded too often of the excellencies of our Lord Jesus Christ. It is only too easy to allow the routine of life with its struggles and trials to keep us 'earthbound'. And yet our great need is to

[1] Owen, *Works*, 8:35.

cultivate heavenly-mindedness. But how are we to do this? Owen's words help us.

The essence of biblical heavenly-mindedness is a mind taken up with the glory of Jesus Christ. One of the (many) benefits of reading men like Owen (and others of his ilk) is that they had expansive views of the greatness and glory of Christ. I am not saying we should yearn for days that are past. Solomon warns us against such folly: 'Do not say, "Why were the old days better than these?" For it is not wise to ask such questions' (*Eccles.* 7:10, NIV). Our calling is not to ape past days, nor to wish wistfully they could return. They are past. However, we can and surely should, long to enjoy the deep spirituality that men like John Owen appeared to enjoy. And at the heart of their deep spirituality were expansive views of the grace and glory of the Saviour.

Samuel Rutherford, a contemporary of Owen, wrote much of the soul-satisfying excellency of Christ:

Oh that I could have leave to look in through the hole of the door, to see His face and sing His praises! or (*sic*) could break up one of His chamber-windows, to look in upon His delighting beauty, till my Lord send more! Any little communion with Him, one of His love-looks, should be my heaven begun . . . I think I see more of Christ than ever I saw; and yet I see but little of what may be seen . . . Oh, His weight, His worth, His sweetness, His overpassing beauty! If men and angels would come and look to that great and princely One, their ebbness could never take up His depth, their narrowness could never comprehend His breadth, height, and length. If ten thousand thousand worlds of angels were created, they might all tire themselves in wondering at His beauty, and begin again to wonder anew.[1]

In another letter he wrote, 'Christ is a well of life; but who knoweth how deep it is to the bottom? . . . And oh, what a fair one, what an only one, what an excellent, lovely, ravishing one is Jesus.' The majesty and loveliness of Christ is the outstanding theme of his letters. For Rutherford, the incomparable loveliness of Christ is the supreme delight of his heart: 'Oh, but Christ is heaven's wonder, and earth's wonder! What marvel that His bride saith, "He is altogether lovely," . . . Oh, pity for evermore, that there should be such a one as Christ Jesus, so boundless, so bottomless, and so incomparable in infinite excellency and sweetness and so few to take him.'

Throughout the ages of eternity, God's people will be 'lost in wonder, love, and praise' as we endlessly worship our great God and King. There can surely, then, be no better preparation for heaven than learning here and now to find our 'all in all' in our Lord Jesus Christ. He is the heavenly manna; he is the living water. Having him we have everything. It is only when we see this world in the light of the incomparable excellencies of our Saviour that we can see through its painted glamour and realise that

[1] Rutherford, *Letters*, pp. 330-331.

> Solid joys and lasting treasure,
> None but Zion's children know.[1]

My friend knew that the best legacy he could leave his wife was the vision of an all-glorious Christ. This he did.

37. The Reminder that Faith Always Needs

Six times in 1 Corinthians 6 Paul wrote, 'Do you not know . . . ?' He was reminding God's people of basic, very basic, Christian truths that they were in danger of forgetting. One of these 'Do you not knows' states, 'Do you not know that the wicked will not inherit the kingdom of God? Do not be deceived . . .' The catalogue of sins that follow makes solemn reading: 'Neither the sexually immoral, nor idolaters, nor adulterers, nor male prostitutes, nor homosexual offenders, nor thieves, nor the greedy, nor drunkards, nor swindlers will inherit the kingdom of God.' Wonderfully, however, Paul continued, 'And that is what some of you were. But you were washed, you were sanctified, you were justified in the name of the Lord Jesus and by the Spirit of our God.'

[1] From John Newton's hymn, 'Glorious things of thee are spoken'.

What is deeply sobering here is that Paul can write to a church he founded, under God, and that he had spent at least a year and a half in, and yet still have to say to them, 'Do you not know that the wicked will not inherit the kingdom of God?' I read recently words that spoke with some power to me: 'A minister's people are never as far along the way as he thinks they are; and he himself is never as far along the way as he thinks he is.' It is only too easy to assume that people who sit under the evangelical, Reformed ministry of God's word, are being decisively shaped and styled by its truth. It may be; but it may not be, at least to the extent we imagine.

You would think that what Paul wrote in 1 Corinthians 6:9-10 would be foundational knowledge for all Christians. How could it be otherwise? Indeed! But the fact is that Paul found it necessary to raise this common, foundational truth with his Corinthian brothers and sisters. The atmosphere of the age exerted a powerful, perhaps even beguiling and desensitising, influence. The permissive society that was ancient Corinth had a way of dulling sensibilities to the sinfulness of sin. When 'everybody is doing it', after a little time we can become, if not anaesthetised to sinful behaviour, less offended by it, less troubled by it, less sensitive to its God-hating, God-denying character.

Paul's list of sins in 1 Corinthians 6:9-11 focus attention on the two great false gods of both first-century Corinth and our own twenty-first century world—sex and money. Unless you consider yourself 'above' being influenced by such sins (and if you did you would be deeply self-deceived—another of Paul's apostolic concerns), you will know how vital it is for every Christian believer, no matter how mature and well read, to 'watch and pray'. We cannot for one moment take for granted that we are immune from certain sins, even some of the grosser sins in Paul's catalogue! Here is a church established by the Apostle Paul. For over eighteen months they have listened to a God-inspired apostle of Christ teach them the word and ways of God. What a wonderfully privileged church this was. And yet, Paul senses the need to speak to them boldly and bluntly about the most awful of sins. Is it not true that those of us who are pastors and preachers are not speaking as basically, as elementally, as pointedly to God's people as we should be?

Our present age is pervaded by an atmosphere of sensual, even hedonistic, indulgence. There is little doubt that evangelicalism is not what it once was. The cutting edge of personal purity and righteous separation from an unholy world is little more than a distant memory. Not for one moment am I advocating 'pietism', a retreat from the world into pious ghettos. No, 'the earth is the LORD's' (*Psa.* 24:1). But our Saviour's prayer in John 17 should surely be to the fore in our own praying: 'I do not ask that you take them out of the world, but that you *keep them from the evil one*. Sanctify them in the truth; your word is truth' (verse 16, 17).

Are we helping our children, our young folk in the church, to live distinctively? The wicked will not inherit the kingdom of God, no matter what ecclesiastical bodies seek to redefine sin and make it less than it really is. None of us are as far along as we think we are. The insidious atmosphere of the age can dull and even all but deaden our spiritual sensibilities. Let us pray that the Lord would impress his truth with renewed power on our hearts and minds. Let us pray for one another that we will not be self-deceived and compromised by the prevailing wickedness. It is not merely a matter of evangelical distinctiveness—eternal destinies are at stake.

38. Jesus Christ: Faith's Obsession

John Brown was one of the most illustrious Bible commentators of the nineteenth century. The Banner of Truth Trust publishes his commentaries on Galatians, 1 Peter, and his three volume work on *The Discourses and Sayings of our Lord*. While recently perusing Brown's *Commentary on 1 Peter*, I came across this wonderful paragraph. He is commenting on the opening verses of 1 Peter 2 and in particular on the Christ-saturated content of these verses:

The religion taught in the New Testament, of which our text is a fair specimen, is Christianity in the most emphatic and peculiar sense of the term, 'Christ is all in all'. It is his religion. It is all by him; it is all about him; he is its author, he is its substance; he is the sum of this system, the soul of this body. Everything is viewed in its connexion with him. Every doctrine and every precept, every privilege and every duty, every promise and every threatening. The ground of acceptance is his sacrifice; the source of light and life, holiness and peace, his Spirit; the rule of duty, his law; the pattern for imitation, his example; the motives to duty, his authority and grace; the great end of all, his glory, God's glory in him . . . let the language of our hearts be that of the dying martyr: 'None but Christ, none but Christ.'

Are these not stirring, moving, and true words?

In essence, Brown is telling us that Christianity is Christ. He is the 'so great salvation' that God holds out to us in the gospel. This was something Jesus himself was self-consciously aware of. When you read through the Gospels you cannot miss that he preaches *himself*. This is seen perhaps most startlingly in Matthew 11:28-30: 'Come to me all you who labour and are heavy laden, and I will give you rest . . .' Jesus does not prescribe for the weary and burdened some spiritual panacea; he prescribes himself. Jesus' personal sense of his comprehensive ability to meet the needs of a broken, sin-weary world is staggering: 'Come to me'!

Why mention the obvious? For one simple reason: to encourage you to look alone to our Lord Jesus for the comfort, help, strength, reassurance, and hope that we all need to sustain us in our walk with God. It is in Christ that God has blessed us with every spiritual blessing (*Eph.* 1:3). God has nothing else to give you, for in his Son he has given you everything. Not just everything you need, but *everything!*

This is but another way of saying what our Lord himself tells us in *John* 15:5, 'I am the vine, you are the branches'. He is our life. To live by faith is to live 'out of Christ' (see *Gal.* 2:20). Faith is like a bucket that we drop into the inexhaustible riches and depths of our Saviour, to draw up out of him all we need to live a godly, God-pleasing, gospel-useful life. Do you lack wisdom? Go to Christ who is the wisdom of God. Do you lack patience? Go to Christ the epitome of godly patience. Do you lack constancy? Go to Christ who was obedient unto death. Do you lack courage? Go to Christ 'who endured the cross'. John Calvin puts this truth beautifully in the *Institutes*

> We see that our whole salvation and all its parts are comprehended in Christ (*Acts* 4:12). We should therefore take care not to derive the least portion of it from anywhere else. If we seek salvation, we are taught by the very name of Jesus that it is 'of him' (*1 Cor.* 1:30). If we seek any other gifts of the Spirit, they will be found in his anointing. If we seek

strength, it lies in his dominion; if purity in his conception; if gentleness, it appears in his birth . . . If we seek redemption, it lies in his passion; if acquittal, in his condemnation; if remission from the curse, in his cross (*Gal.* 3:13) . . . In short, since rich store of every kind of good abounds in him, let us drink our fill from this fountain, and from no other.[1]

Now that is theology at its most biblical and glorious! Ponder that. Thank God for that. Live in the great good of all that Jesus Christ is.

39. *Faith's Supreme Interest*

Some verses in the Bible are deeply disturbing, and unexpected. As Paul commends Timothy to the church in Philippi, he tells them, 'I have no one like him [of like soul], who will be genuinely concerned for your welfare' (*Phil.* 2:20). So far, so good. But then Paul continues, 'For they all seek their own interests, not those of Jesus Christ' (verse 21). Are these not surprising and perplexing words? Even if Paul is generalising (he later warmly commends faithful, life-risking Epaphroditus to the Philippians), what he says is deeply disturbing.

[1] Calvin, *Institutes*, 2.16.19.

Paul is in prison, probably in Rome. In 1:15ff. he tells us that some in Rome were preaching 'Christ from envy and rivalry', seeking to 'afflict me in my imprisonment' (1:17). Now he tells us that 'they all seek their own interests, not those of Jesus Christ'. These are salutary words.

It is only too easy to deceive ourselves into thinking that, while we are not the Christians we should be, we would never sink so low as to put our own interests above and before those of our Lord Jesus. My brothers and sisters, it is only too easy to drift along in the Christian life, becoming increasingly conformed to the world around us, yet hardly being aware of our condition. In the context of Paul's words, the interests of Jesus Christ are equated with Timothy's genuine concern for the welfare of the Philippian believers. Like his Lord and Saviour, Timothy put the concerns and well-being of God's people before his own interests. The mind of Christ (see *Phil.* 2:5ff.) was stamped on Timothy's mind and resulted in a selfless care and concern for others. This is what Paul hardly saw in anyone else: 'they all seek their own interests'!

There is no escaping the teaching of our Lord Jesus that it will be, and is, costly to follow him. He invites us, indeed summons us, to take up our cross and follow him. He calls us to 'seek first God's kingdom and his righteousness'. He tells us, 'By this all people will know that you are my disciples, if you have love one for the other' (*John* 13:35). John must have drunk deeply of

Jesus' teaching because he later wrote, 'We know that we have passed out of death into life, because we love the brothers . . . Little children, let us not love in word or talk, but in deed and in truth' (*1 John* 3:14, 18).

One of the pre-eminent interests of our Lord Jesus Christ is the care of his 'little flock'. He loves his lambs and gently leads those that have young. He seeks to show his care and compassion through the self-denying kindness and practical care of his people. But (and it is a huge 'but'), the truth is that we can become so wrapped up in ourselves, in our situations, in our own concerns and cares (albeit legitimate), that we neglect the brotherhood (see *1 Pet.* 2:17).

Whose interests do you and I live for? When did we last disturb our own comfort and go out of our way to minister the Saviour's kindness to our fellow struggling believers? Why not stop now and write a letter of encouragement, put on your coat and make a surprise visit, send flowers, pray, pick up the phone, or whatever, and make someone's day.

Earlier this year I received a letter from someone I have never met. From the writing (yes, it was hand-written, something of a rarity today) I assume it was from an older man. His letter was an out-of-the-blue encouragement to me. Wouldn't it be good and honouring to our Saviour if we could all do something that would minister his kindness and care to his 'little flock'? Timothy sought the interests of Jesus Christ.

40. Faith's Unsettling Obsessiveness

Paul must have been an unsettling companion. For him the Christian life could never be lived by half measures. He was an all or nothing man. The gospel of God's grace in Christ had not only captured him, it had captivated him. He counted everything (yes, *everything*) as loss because of the surpassing worth of knowing Christ Jesus his Lord (*Phil*. 3:8). This 'gospel obsession' with Christ made Paul a one-thing-I-do man. Having acknowledged to the Philippians that he was not yet perfect, that he had not yet 'arrived', Paul exclaimed, 'But one thing I do: forgetting what lies behind and straining forward to what lies ahead, I press on toward the goal for the prize of the upward call of God in Christ Jesus' (*Phil*. 3:13, 14).

'One thing I do'! When I was a young divinity student at Edinburgh University, I worshipped at Holyrood Abbey Church of Scotland, where James Philip was the minister. I remember, as if it were yesterday, Jim bending over the pulpit and quietly, but powerfully, saying to the many young people in the congregation, 'Are you a one-thing-I-do man, a one-thing-I-do woman?' 'One thing I do'. Paul did many things, but in all the things he did there was one thing he was always doing. He was always pressing on 'toward the goal for the prize of the upward call of God in Christ Jesus'. For Paul, the life of faith in Jesus Christ meant that he longed to be with his Lord and Saviour. There was an inerradicable heavenly-mindedness to Paul's faith. Earlier in Philippians 1:23, he told the church that his present desire was 'to depart and be with Christ, for that is better'.

'One thing I do'. This is easier to say than to do; easier to preach than to do. Paul seems to be conscious of this. Immediately following these words he says, 'forgetting what lies behind'. Paul knows that there are 'former things' that can hold us back and keep us from becoming one-thing-I-do men and women. There are former sins, perhaps grievous and glaring sins. The devil will do all he can to keep you in some kind of thrall to former sins. He will seek to keep you so ashamed of them that you can never forget them, and they end up haunting you all your life.

There is a sense, of course, in which we should never forget what we once were, that we might the more magnify the great grace of God that came to us in Christ and saved us. Paul told Timothy, 'formerly I was a blasphemer, persecutor, and insolent opponent' of Christ and the gospel (*1 Tim.* 1:13). But God had mercy on him. He was a new man in Christ (2 *Cor.* 5:17), God had remembered his sins no more, buried them in the deepest sea, and removed them from him as far as the east is from the west. This is a good kind of remembering. But there is a remembering of 'former things' that is far from healthy. They continue to haunt us, like a dark cloud that seems always to be there. Only when the gospel of God's forgiving, restoring love in Christ rescues us from the tyranny of 'former things' can we begin to be one-thing-I-do men and women.

I said earlier that there was an inerradicable heavenly-mindedness about Paul. It was this heavenly-mindedness that defined the shape of his Christian life. In all he was and did, Paul pressed on 'toward the goal for the prize of the upward call of God in Christ Jesus' (*Phil.* 3:14). He had no intention of ambling his way to glory. Like a compelling magnet, the eternal glories drew him onward and upward.

It was said of Richard Sibbes, the Cambridge Puritan, that heaven was in him before he was in heaven. So it was with Paul. You are not to imagine that Sibbes, or even Paul for that matter, were unusual men. Paul called himself 'the chief of sinners'. What made these two men, and myriad others like them, obsessed with Christ and the heavenly glory, was their resolve to 'seek the things that are above, where Christ is, seated at the right hand of God' (*Col.* 3:1). They were so spiritually dazzled by the grace and glory of Christ that everything else seemed almost insipid to them. They had tasted that the Lord is good (*Psa.* 34:8) and they longed constantly to feed on his flesh and drink his blood (*John* 6:54-58 — while these words may reflect the communion with Christ that lies at the heart of the Lord's supper, their main import is to centre the life of faith in the Lord Jesus' atoning sacrifice and the rich benefits that flow to us through our faith-union with our Saviour).

Does all this seem too intense, too serious, too much? Well, compared to Paul and Richard Sibbes our lives may seem lacking in every way. But is it not your heart's desire to be a one-thing-I-do man, woman? Do you not long to say with Paul, 'I count everything as loss because of the surpassing worth of knowing Christ Jesus my Lord'? (*Phil.* 3:8). If not, I suggest you have serious questions to ask yourself. Our Lord Jesus once spoke these deeply searching words: 'Whoever loves father or mother more than me is not worthy of me; and whoever loves son or daughter more than me is not worthy of me' (*Matt.* 10:37). So, it all comes down to this: What value do you place upon the Lord Jesus Christ? The value you place on him will be the measure you live for him.

41. *Faith's Assurance: 'Nothing So Ill but Christ Will Compensate'*

The Christian life is lived at the intersection of the ages—this present age and the age of the world to come that has already, in Christ, punctuated this present age. In Christ, believers are a 'new creation' (*2 Cor.* 5:17). Paul does not mean here that believers are inwardly renewed men and women, but that we have been planted by God into the midst of the new creation that he has effected in Christ. This 'intersection of the ages' accounts, in part, for the tension that every Christian experiences as he or she labours to 'seek first the kingdom of God and his righteousness' (*Matt.* 6:33). It is an inevitable tension, an unavoidable tension, but in the wisdom and mercy of God a sanctifying tension.

The words at the head of this chapter were written by John Owen. They reflect his conviction that 'for those who love God all things work together for good' (*Rom.* 8:28). Paul begins that verse with, 'And we know . . .' He is not engaging in spiritual conjecture or surmising. He is not saying, 'we know that some things, or perhaps even many things, work for the good of those who love God'. Paul is unequivocal, 'we know that . . . all things work together for good, for those who are called according to his purpose'. These are staggering words, remarkable words, almost unimaginable words. But they are written in the word of the One who cannot lie.

In recent months I have found myself engaged in lives that have known great sorrow, disappointment, illness, and death. John Calvin spoke for many when he wrote,

> Our circumstances are all in opposition to the promises of God. He promises us immortality, yet we are surrounded by mortality and corruption. He declares that he accounts us just, yet we are covered

with sins. He testifies that he is propitious and benevolent towards us, yet outward signs threaten his wrath. What then are we to do?

Indeed, what then are we to do? Too often we go into a 'spiritual sulk' and blame God for not ordering our life the way we think it should be ordered. But, in your saner moments, would you really want God to order your life the way *you* want it ordered? If you did, you would be a poor self-deceived, even Satan-deceived, fool! Do *you* know what is best for you? Do *you* know the end from the beginning? Are *you* the fount of all wisdom? At best we 'see through a glass darkly'. We need the loving-kindness and tender fatherly care of our heavenly King, to keep us on track, preparing us for the glory that we will one day inherit (and even now are beginning to enjoy).

Let me now give you Calvin's own answer to the question he posed.

> What then are we to do? We must close our eyes, disregard ourselves and all things connected with us, so that nothing may hinder or prevent us from believing that God is true.[1]

Calvin was absolutely sure, how could he be otherwise, that there is

> Nothing so ill but Christ will compensate.

---

[1] Calvin, *Commentaries*, on Romans 4:20.

The great issue is not, are you willing to believe what God's word teaches? But, are you willing to believe the goodness, grace, loving-kindness of your heavenly Father? Jesus laboured to impress on his disciples the loving Fatherhood of their God (read *Matt.* 6 and see how many times Jesus speaks of the '*Father*'). This is the issue we need to settle in our minds and hearts: Am I persuaded that my heavenly Father is everything he tells me he is? This is the battle of faith, a battle that will throw the concerted powers and seductions of the world, the flesh, and the devil against you.

Perhaps you have gone through, or are going through, dark and difficult times. Allow me to encourage you to take Owen's words to heart. See them through the bright lens of Romans 8:28. Hide that word in your heart that you might not sin against God (*Psa.* 119:11). Live in the faith of this and, to quote Owen again, 'Thou wilt die a conqueror'.

42. *Thinking Faith: The Logic of Redemption*

The glorious doctrine of God's redemption of sinners through the sin-bearing, sin-vanquishing death of Christ on Calvary's cross lies at the heart of the Christian Faith—and at the heart of every Christian's faith. We believe this. We love this. We sing this. 'In him we have redemption through his blood, the forgiveness of our trespasses, according to the riches of his grace' (*Eph.* 1:7). So far, so good. Now consider this question: What impact and influence is Christ's redeeming work to have on our relationships with other Christians?

The New Testament is emphatic that there is a vital, inextricable link between what our Saviour has done for us and how we are to treat one another. Listen to the Apostle John: 'Beloved, if God so loved us [in giving his Son as a propitiation for our sins], we also ought to love one another' (*1 John* 4:11). For John there is logic to redemption, the logic of selfless love for others. If God in Christ has loved us selflessly, and he has, how can we partake of that selfless love and not exhibit something of its grace in our relationships with others?

This is no arcane question. Our Lord Jesus said 'by their fruit you will know them'. He also said that love for one another would be the distinguishing mark of our Christian profession. This is the logic of redemption. Where this is absent, the experience of redeeming love can hardly be present—can it?

It has often been said that just as everything in Christianity *flows from* the cross, so everything *returns to* the cross. It is when we become distant and detached from the wonder of Calvary's redeeming love that we become careless, even indifferent in our relationships with fellow believers. It would transform the way we speak about other Christians and to other Christians if we always did so 'in the shadow of Calvary'. The self-less love of Christ is both the foundation and pulsebeat of the Christian life. The mark of the Selfless One has been indelibly etched on the life of every Christian. What the Holy Spirit first produced in Christ he comes to reproduce in his people.

The Apostle John learnt this well: 'By this we know love, that he laid down his life for us, and we ought to lay down our lives for the brothers' (*1 John* 3:16). This kind of Christianity is light years away from what passes as Christian in this world. It would be only too easy to look out and see and point the finger at the lovelessness in the liberal, unbelieving church. But what about us, we who call ourselves evangelical and Reformed? Does the logic of redemption pervade our relationships with one another? Well, does it?

It is not a merely matter of trying harder, although we need to try much harder. It is a matter of becoming soaked in the logic of redemption. We all need day by day to come afresh to the foot of Calvary's cross—not to gaze upon a dying Saviour (for he is risen!), but to be reminded of the selfless love that purchased our redemption at a cost we will never be able to fathom. Is this not our great need?

43. *Faith's Constant Companion*

Every Christian has been 'created in Christ Jesus for good works' (*Eph.* 2:10). So much are good works native and necessary to authentic Christian faith, that the Apostle James tells us that 'faith by itself, if it does not have works, is dead' (*James* 2:17). In saying this, James is simply echoing the teaching of our Lord Jesus Christ. When Jesus warned his disciples to 'beware of false prophets', he told them that they could be recognised as false prophets by the fruit their lives produced: 'every healthy tree bears good fruit, but the diseased tree bears bad fruit . . . Every tree that does not bear good fruit is cut down and thrown into the fire. Thus you will recognise them by their fruits' (*Matt.* 7:15-20). No biblically taught Christian will dispute this.

The question that naturally arises at this point, however, is a pressing one: God has created me in Christ Jesus for good works, but my good works are inconsistent, lacking, and shot through with pride, mere dutifulness, and often half-heartedness. How then can I ever be acceptable to God, who is 'of purer eyes than to see evil and cannot look at wrong' (*Hab.* 1:13)? Even when I have done all that I can do, all that God has commanded me to do, the Lord himself confirms that I am yet 'an unprofitable servant' (cf. *Luke* 17:10).

There are some men today, within Reformed churches, for whom this is no dilemma at all. They teach that, notwithstanding our sinfully defective good works, God accepts what we give to him and justifies us through faith in Christ and the good works that are intrinsic to true faith. At first sight there is a plausibility about this new teaching (though it echoes in its major points the teaching of the Council of Trent in the 1540s). Throughout the Scriptures both the graces and good works of believers are declared to be acceptable to God. Peter tells us that 'the imperishable beauty of a gentle and quiet spirit' is 'very precious in God's sight' (*1 Pet.* 3:4); the writer to the Hebrews tells us that the continual offering up of 'a sacrifice of praise', doing good and sharing what we have are 'pleasing to God' (*Heb.* 13:15, 16); Paul confirms that the sacrificial gifts of God's people are a 'sacrifice acceptable and pleasing to God' (*Phil.* 4:18); finally, our Lord Jesus Christ says that 'Whoever receives a prophet because he is a prophet will receive a prophet's reward . . . And whoever gives one of these little ones even a cup of cold water because he is a disciple, truly, I say to you, he will by no means lose his reward' (*Matt.* 10:41-42). It is not difficult, therefore, to see that 'good works' belong to the heart of the Christian Faith, are acceptable to God because in accordance with his revealed will, and are the fruit of the indwelling Holy Spirit. But how do these 'good works' relate to the believer's justification? Do they, in any measure, contribute towards his justification? The

Scriptures answer this question unequivocally: Good works are the effect of faith and the visible evidence of our justification; they have no part to play in the faith that is the instrumental means of our justification. As such, 'good works' do not, and cannot, form any part of the ground or basis of our justification—'Since we have been justified by faith, we have peace with God through our Lord Jesus Christ' (*Rom.* 5:1; cf. 4:5).

Yet, the good works of believers are truly acceptable to God—but only through the merit of Christ. James Buchanan makes the point well:

> Considered as fruits of our sanctification . . . [good works] cannot be too highly commended; but considered as the ground of our Justification, or as forming any part of our TITLE to that inheritance, they are to be utterly rejected, and treated as 'dung' and 'filthy rags' with reference to that end; for they cannot be regarded as such, without dishonour to the redeeming work of Christ; and for this reason the Apostle, speaking of himself as having been, 'as touching the righteousness which is in the law, blameless', declares that he had renounced all dependence upon it, and upon everything else but Christ alone' (quoting *Phil.* 3:9).[1]

How then are we to assess recent teaching that maintains that we are justified by obedient faith (in the sense

---

[1] James Buchanan, *The Doctrine of Justification* (Edinburgh: Banner of Truth, 1984), pp. 363-4.

that acts of obedience are inherent in our faith), and not by faith alone in Jesus Christ? This revisionist teaching (it is a contradiction of the Reformation consensus on justification) is seriously flawed in at least two ways.

First, it over-estimates the character of the good works a believer can perform and under-estimates what is pleasing and acceptable to our thrice holy God. Put more bluntly: How much obedience must I give for God, along with my faith in Christ, to justify me? Must it be wholly consistent, or will intermittent obedience be sufficient? And what about the quality of my believing obedience? What measure of qualitative obedience will God consider acceptable? These are not obtuse questions.

Second, this 'Reformed revisionism' is even more seriously flawed: It profoundly fails to understand the significance of our Lord Jesus Christ's earthly obedience. If my ultimate acceptance with God rests upon Christ's atoning work on the cross and on my good works, what becomes of the saving significance of Christ's humanity from Bethlehem to Calvary? Is the significance of his life from the Virgin's womb to being nailed to the cross merely a prelude to the main event, as it were? Are we only to understand Jesus' obedience as what was necessary for him to be the sinless offering that would take away the sin of the world? In this connection, it is vastly significant that Paul can describe the whole course of Jesus' life, death, and resurrection as 'one act of righteousness [that] leads to justification and life for all men' (*Rom.* 5:18). For Paul, the 'active obedience' of Christ and the 'passive obedience' of Christ, are *one* obedience. As he puts it in Philippians 2:8, Jesus was 'obedient to the point of death, even death on a cross'. The saving obedience of Christ encompassed every phase of his earthly, mediatorial life. In Romans 5:18ff., Paul understands the whole course of our Saviour's life in terms of representative headship—what the One did had saving implications for all men. Our standing before God rests alone on Christ's 'one act of righteousness', which God imputes to our account by faith alone (*Rom.* 5:18, 19).

John Bunyan tells us in his book *Grace Abounding* of his own discovery of this glorious truth:

> I was all this while ignorant of Jesus Christ; and going about to establish my own righteousness; and had perished therein, had not God in mercy showed me more of my state by nature . . . But one day, as I was passing into the field . . . suddenly this sentence fell upon my soul, Thy righteousness is in heaven; and methought, withal, I saw with the eyes of my soul, Jesus Christ at God's right hand: there, I say, was my righteousness; so that wherever I was, or whatever I was doing, God could not say of me, He wants [lacks] My righteousness; for that was just before him. I also saw moreover, that it was not my good frame of heart that made my righteousness better, nor yet my bad frame that made my righteousness worse; for my righteousness was

Jesus Christ himself . . . Now did my chains fall off my legs indeed; I was loosed from my afflictions and irons . . . now went I also home rejoicing, for the grace and love of God.[1]

The deeply flawed teaching which maintains that 'the personal godliness of the believer is also necessary for his justification in the judgment of the last day' and that 'abiding in Christ by keeping his commandments . . . are all necessary for continuing in the state of justification' (as a leading exponent of this new teaching has written) needs to be seen for what it is, a regression into moralism and Romanism.

It is remarkable how this new teaching seeks to trace its heritage back to the Reformers. Calvin for one, however, is absolutely clear what the ground of our justification is and what significance the good works of believers have. In a lecture on Ezekiel 18:17,[2] Calvin explains how the doctrine, 'faith without works justifies', is either true or false, depending on the sense it bears. He explains,

[1] John Bunyan, *Grace Abounding to the Chief of Sinners* (London, 1905, ed), pp. 32, 129-130.

[2] I was directed to this quote from Calvin by Dr Mark Garcia. It is found in his doctoral thesis: *Life in Christ: The Function of Union with Christ in the 'Unio-Duplex Gratia' Structure of Calvin's Soteriology with Special Reference to the Relationship of Justification and Sanctification in Sixteenth-Century Context* (Ph.D. thesis, Edinburgh, 2004).

But although works tend in no way to be the cause of justification, yet, when the elect sons of God were justified freely by faith, at the same time their works are esteemed righteous by the same gratuitous liberality. Thus it remains true that faith without works justifies, although this needs prudence and a sound interpretation. For this proposition, 'faith without works justifies,' is true and yet false, according to different senses. 'Faith without works justifies when by itself' is false, because faith without works is void (*nulla est*). But if the clause 'without works' is joined with the word 'to justify,' the proposition will be true: therefore faith cannot justify when it is without works, because it is dead, and a mere fiction (*merum figmentum*). He who is born of God is just, as John says (*1 John* 5:18). Thus faith can be no more separated from works than the sun from its heat yet faith justifies without works, because works do not form a reason (*rationem*) for our justification; but faith alone (*sola fides*) reconciles us to God and causes him to love us, not in ourselves, but in his only begotten Son.

This has ever been the Reformed understanding of the relationship between the believer's faith and good works. Any other construction confuses justification and sanctification, makes the believer a contributor to his justification, and denies the saving significance of Christ's active obedience.

Shortly before he died, J. Gresham Machen sent his

colleague and dear friend John Murray a telegram with these words, 'I'm so thankful for the active obedience of Christ. No hope without it.' This alone is how anyone can stand before God on the great day of Jesus Christ, cleansed by the Saviour's blood and clothed with his imputed righteousness. This is where faith rests, on the perfect righteousness of Jesus Christ. He *alone* is our hope. He has done it *all*.

Also published by the Trust

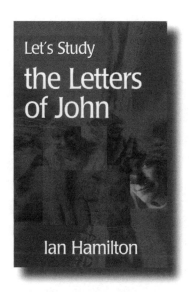

Let's Study the Letters of John

Ian Hamilton

ISBN: 978 1 84871 013 9

paperback, 144pp.

Like much of the New Testament, John's three letters were written to deal with pressing difficulties being experienced in the first-century churches. False teachers, whom John calls 'antichrists', were denying fundamental Christian truths and deeply troubling the Christians whom the aged apostle loved and called his 'little children'. John writes with warmth, seriousness, and urgency to correct this situation. He shows that sound doctrine is vital, not only to the well-being of Christians, but to their very existence, since error leads to deception, darkness, and ultimately the destruction of those who embrace it.

The message of John's letters is of perennial relevance, and especially important in our own day. Ian Hamilton's concise commentary provides a warmly pastoral explanation of John's timeless message, pointing the reader to the Word made flesh, the Lord Jesus Christ, as the answer to all problems in the church, whether in the first or the twenty-first century.

The Banner of Truth Trust originated in 1957 in London. The founders believed that much of the best literature of historic Christianity had been allowed to fall into oblivion and that, under God, its recovery could well lead not only to a strengthening of the church today but to true revival.

Inter-denominational in vision, this publishing work is now international, and our lists include a number of contemporary authors along with classics from the past. The translation of these books into many languages is encouraged.

A monthly magazine, *The Banner of Truth*, is also published. More information about this and all our publications can be found on our website or supplied by either of the offices below.

THE BANNER OF TRUTH TRUST

3 Murrayfield Road
Edinburgh, EH12 6EL
UK

PO Box 621, Carlisle
Pennsylvania 17013,
USA

www.banneroftruth.co.uk